THE CLEAR GUIDE TO INVESTING YOUR MONEY IN THE STOCK MARKET

HOW TO PICK WINNING STOCKS AND INCREASE YOUR NET WORTH, FROM TODAY!

CHRIS CHILLINGWORTH

First Published in Great Britain 2019

Copyright © Chris Chillingworth

All rights reserved. No part of this publication may be reproduced, stored in or introduced into a retrieval system, or transmitted, in any form, or by any means (electronic, mechanical, photocopying, recording or otherwise) without the prior written permission of the publisher.

The right of Chris Chillingworth to be identified as the authors of this work has been asserted by them in accordance with the Copyright, Designs and Patents Act 1988.

This book is sold subject to the condition that it shall not, by any way of trade or otherwise, be lent, resold, hired out, or otherwise circulated without the publisher's prior consent in any form of binding or cover other than that in which it is published and without a similar condition including this condition being imposed on the subsequent purchaser.

ISBN-13: 978-1916190924

CONTENTS

INTRODUCTION		1
CHAPTER 1	THE RESULTS	5
CHAPTER 2	9 GUIDING PRINCIPLES TO INVESTING IN STOCKS	11
CHAPTER 3	MITIGATING THE RISK	15
CHAPTER 4	MY INVESTING PHILOSOPHY	23
	WHY YOU CAN'T PREDICT SHORT TERM MARKETS	25
	HOW TO PUT THE ODDS IN YOUR FAVOUR	29
	THE NOISE OF THE MARKETS	37
	KEEPING THINGS SIMPLE	49
CHAPTER 5	WHY INVEST?	53
	ASSETS & LIABILITIES	55
	BUY YOUR STOCKS LIKE YOU BUY YOUR GROCERIES	59
	UNDERSTANDING DIVIDENDS	61
	UNDERSTANDING EX-DIVIDEND DATES	63
	UNDERSTANDING DIVIDEND YIELDS	65
	CONCERNS WITH DIVIDEND INVESTING	67
	COMPOUNDED INTEREST	69
CHAPTER 6	ANALYSIS OF A FTSE COMPANY	73
	BUILDING THE CRITERIA	75
	WHAT I'M LOOKING FOR	79
	REVENUE	81
	GROSS PROFIT	87
	EXPENSES	89
	RESEARCH & DEVELOPMENT	91
	DEPRECIATION & AMORTISATION	93
	INTEREST ON DEBT/FINANCE	95
	NET EARNINGS	97
	LIQUIDITY	99
	RESERVES	101
	BUYING BACK SHARES	103
	RETURN ON SHAREHOLDER EQUITY	105
	CONSISTENCY	107
	FINANCIAL SUMMARIES & WHY I DON'T USE THEM	109

CHAPTER 7 THE WATCHLIST	123
CHAPTER 8 THE STRATEGY	**129**
MY STRATEGY	131
BUY AND HOLD	133
GETTING IN AT THE RIGHT PRICE	137
THE FEAR OF MARKET CRASHES	139
FACTORING IN COMMISSION CHARGES	143
ASSET ALLOCATION	145
MY ASSET ALLOCATION RULE OF THUMB	147
CHAPTER 9 THE SUCCESSES	**149**
HALMA PLC	153
SAGE GROUP PLC	154
DIPLOMA PLC	155
MJ GLEESON PLC	156
AB DYNAMICS PLC	157
CONTACT THE AUTHOR	**159**

INTRODUCTION

I use a rigorous and mechanical process for picking my stocks. It involves a depth of analysis that can take me anywhere from 2-3 hours per stock. From there the process is one of ongoing two-step maintenance.

1) Ensuring these companies are still meeting the criteria each quarter

2) Checking whether the ones which previously failed have since become eligible.

Most companies fail my analysis. They do not make the grade. Many household names and big brands fail the test.

The companies that fail the test are not companies I invest in. Only a select few stocks make the grade. It is only in these companies I invest my money. I explain more about how I find these companies later within this book.

In a moment, however, I want to show you the actual results my portfolio of companies has achieved going back as far as 2014.

Of course, over this time, companies have come and gone. The portfolio is dynamic in that it can change as new companies are added to it, and some are removed each year.

These are the exact results of the stocks in the portfolio at the time. They reflect the performance achieved by my overall strategy towards stock identification and implementation.

Each of the following years has been compared against the overall market. The FTSE 100 plays the part of the benchmark. If you have not been able to beat the overall market performance, then this is a perfect sign that you should probably stop you investment activities immediately. Instead, take stock of what you're doing before continuing (if you'll pardon the pun).

If your strategy performs worse than the FTSE index, then essentially whatever you're doing is costing you money, not adding to the established baseline.

I have met many traders this year, for instance, who report having lost significant capital on the stock market. This has happened in a year when simply investing your capital on the FTSE 100 would have achieved you a 10% return on investment.

These losing investors and traders would have lost nothing, and instead made money just buying a FTSE 100 index fund and making 10%.

This year I've spoken to traders who walked away 60% down this year. Their systems and strategies are often cumbersome and complicated. There is a real trend for trying to be overly clever and predict markets. There is also a real trend for boosting one's ego and putting more emphasis on being right rather than making money.

One would be forgiven for assuming the two come hand in hand. But in my experience, this is not the case.

If a trader lost 10%, 20% or even 60% trading his/her system this year, using complicated algorithms, a vast array of indicators and a focus on trying to predict what was going to happen, then they're merely getting in their own way of success. Especially when owning a slice of the overall market would have provided a +10% return.

Of course, I am not recommending that you do that. The FTSE has only grown by 8% overall in the last five years. Buying and holding the FTSE 100 is a weak investment plan. It could be an ideal 'low-hanging fruit' solution for those pouring their own money down the drain every year trying to 'master' the markets, however.

I do find it fascinating that so many traders and investors tell me that making good profitable returns is their aim. Yet their actions suggest otherwise when they insist on spending multiple years *"building their own system"* because using someone else's system *"feels like cheating myself"*.

I'd argue that their romantic view of how they want to make money on the markets is what's cheating them.

Trading and investing in the financial stock market is incredibly simple and straightforward these days. We assume that adding layers of complication improves a system. Yet the factual historical trading data that I've read shows the exact opposite. The more 'touches' a trader and investor make, the fewer returns they often achieve.

Much of my research and years crunching the raw numbers suggests that you will make more money by just buying a stock and riding it upwards over the years.

All the entries and exits, the trying to time the markets and trade like a sniper, ends up costing you more than if you'd just bought and held.

Anyone can get that data and find this out for themselves. Which goes to show just how blinkered we traders and investors can be when trying to fine-tune our systems.

This book is dedicated to showing you the reader just how uncomplicated investing in the stock market needs to be to make fantastic profits. I hope you enjoy the ride.

CHAPTER 1
THE RESULTS

PERFORMANCE

2014 (+6%)

A relatively dull year in which the overall FTSE 100 fell from 6749 to 6566 (-3%). The portfolio performance was buoyed by share price growth in both Sage Group plc which rose from £4.05 to £4.65 a share (+15%) and Halma plc which rose from £6.13 to £6.88 (+12%). One other stock in the portfolio also achieved a +34% rise from May to December.

Out of 19 stocks in the portfolio this year, 13 went up, and 6 went down. A winning year when the overall index fell is a testament to my stock selection criteria working fantastically well.

2015 (+28%)

A superb year for the portfolio despite the overall FTSE 100 index falling -5% from 6566 to 6242. Fortunately, many of the portfolio stocks performed fantastically against the global index trend.

Once again, Sage Group plc saw a rise from £4.65 to £5.98 (+29%), and Halma plc rose from £6.88 to £8.52 (+24%). Stand out performer this year however was AB Dynamics, which rose from £1.54 to £3.43 a share. A rise of +123%. MJ Gleeson also went up +54%.

2016 (+11%)

A year that witnessed the FTSE achieve some of it's best

gains from 6242 to 7142 (+14%). The portfolio performed well and almost kept up with Sage Group and Halma plc again contributing to overall gains and AB Dynamics rising +59%. However, with two other stocks dropping -26% and -23% respectively, the results couldn't quite match the index.

Overall, however, by this point, we were well ahead of the FTSE 100 performance 2014-2016, and 11% was a respectable return that year.

2017 (+38%)

One stock achieved a 15% jump in January, a 16% jump in June and a further 11% rise in August, all contributing to a stellar +104% increase in share price value across 2017.

Another pick of mine did not join the watchlist until it qualified in June 2017. It immediately achieved a +23% increase in value followed by a +33% increase the following month in July. Then, going on to deliver a +21% increase in September, +15% in October and +25% in December, resulting in an overall increase in share price value of +182% in 2017.

Only 1 stock across the entire 24 stock portfolio failed to rise in value across 2017, giving the portfolio a 95.9% win rate for the year.

The FTSE 100 achieved a +8% increase in value that year, meaning that once again the portfolio smashed the overall index performance.

2018 (-8%)

2018 was a losing year for both the overall market and the

portfolio.

However, picking the best-performing companies had a positive effect. While some of the stocks did poorly, losing 50% and 33% in value respectively, this was balanced by several shares which had great years. AB Dynamics plc which again rose another +35% this year and another constituent rising +29% in value.

Overall, however, the portfolio still fell by -8%. I am pleased we have again beaten the overall FTSE market, however, which fell by -12%.

2019 (+29% at time of publishing)

Now 27 stocks steady, the portfolio has returned to winning ways. We must wait now, however, to find out how much. It seems unlikely we will lose the +29% gained overall as we are now in very late November with just weeks to go before we draw 2019 to a close and record a 5th winning year from 6. I am pleased to have once again beaten the overall FTSE 100 index which is so far up +10% YTD.

YEAR	PORTFOLIO	FTSE
2014	+6%	-3%
2015	+28%	-5%
2016	+11%	+14%
2017	+38%	+8%
2018	-8%	-12%
2019	+29%	+10%
TOTAL	+104%	+12%

CHAPTER 2
9 GUIDING PRINCIPLES TO INVESTING IN STOCKS

These are my overarching rules that I follow which accompany my strategy and overall approach to investing in the stock market. I will discuss these core rules in more detail throughout this book. However, this list can serve as an easy reference to beginner investors looking to make substantial amounts of money over their lifetime.

1. Don't focus too much on the price you get in at. Whether you paid £3.50 a share or £3.25 won't matter 5-10 years down the line when the price is up far higher.

2. Buy shares like you buy your groceries, every month, whether the price is up or down.

3. Be prepared to hold for a minimum of five years

4. Build your portfolio of assets slowly, over the years, brick by brick.

5. Have a broad understanding of the PLC's main business activity – one which makes sense to you

6. Seek traditional companies with an established record of profitability, consistency and opportunity for growth.

7. Avoid mining and exploration stocks that survive on yearly investments until they strike big. They are too risky.

8. Focus on companies who run efficiently relative to their revenue.

9. Focus on the facts, not people's opinions.

CHAPTER 3
MITIGATING THE RISK

HOW TO MITIGATE THE RISKS

Investing in the stock market has a particular stigma attached to it. Everyone knows someone who knows someone who lost money trying it. It's considered risky and dangerous by those on the outside looking in. However, these old stories, passed from friend to friend over many years, are the stories that end up keeping many people from ever venturing into the world of investing in stocks.

Now, some of the horror stories are true, of course. That friend of yours did indeed have a friend who pumped their money into some random stock they thought was a winner and ended up losing £20,000 on the markets.

It probably did happen.

I have met countless others in my years of doing this who came to me for help after diving in headfirst and losing all their money.

Here's the thing. If you're going to jump in with both feet, have your pockets stuffed with all the cash you have, you'd have better get yourself some training. Because investing in stocks is not just as simple as buying shares in your favourite companies which you like the sound of and expecting the best.

I know people who lost thousands in Woolworths, Debenhams, Thomas Cook, HMV, Game, British Airways, and many other companies who back in the '90s were the forefront of the FTSE index, and today just 20-30 years on, are no longer around.

One friend of mine invested heavily in HMV and Game. He did so just as the digital download and on-demand culture began. It was a massive shift in consumption habits by everyday customers. People had stopped buying DVD's and were starting to download movies instead. Illegally at first, but then via dedicated platforms such as iTunes (Apple), Xbox (Microsoft), Sky, Amazon and Netflix. People were struggling to sell their unwanted DVD's at boot fairs for more than £1 each. No one wanted them anymore.

The same thing had happened to CD's just years beforehand.

When you can download the album you want for £7.99 and get it instantly, and then access it from any device in your home, including your mobile phone, why go to the shops and buy a CD of the same music, which costs £11.99 and can only be played on a dedicated player?

Today it's moved further, and for just £7.99 a month you can have access to almost every song ever made via Spotify, and for £8.99 you can have access to every film ever released via companies like Amazon and Netflix.

Indeed, HMV and Game, companies who sold hard copies of videos, music and computer games would have only survived had they seen it coming early and adapted to the changing times.

They didn't, however, and so they died.

And neither did my friend who invested in both companies quite late.

When I asked him why he chose those particular stocks, his answer was standard for many beginner investors I've met.

"Because I liked them both. I shopped in both of them, and I

love music and games".

If you want to be a successful investor, you will not survive long by picking stocks based on the places you like to shop, nor the industries you enjoy the most.

It is a somewhat amateur approach born from not knowing any better, and it's one of several reasons people lose money. These people then often spend the rest of their lives warning friends, family and loved ones to stay well away from the markets.

While it'll be hard for some to hear, it is often their fault.

But it's not just stocks where investors can make huge errors in judgement.

I often hear about investors who lost everything when they invested in property. Investing in deprived areas of decline, or getting stuck with non-paying tenants whose human rights meant the owner couldn't get them out for nine months, which means 9 months of mortgage payments to be paid solely by the investor with no income to cover.

One friend of mine who ventured into building a property portfolio ended up in a legal battle which cost him thousands of pounds to evict a policeman tenant who had refused to pay rent for six months. Proving that anyone can become a lousy tenant no matter how well you vet them.

I've seen someone pump all their saved up capital into building a coffee shop that spent six months empty every morning because they were in the wrong street with no footfall or passing trade. I spent weeks buying my coffee in there, purely because I felt terrible for him. I was often the only customer in there. The whole time I sat there by the front window nursing my coffee, I never saw a soul walk past or look in. No one knew they were there.

He and his wife had put their heart and soul into what they were doing but got the fundamentals all wrong. A couple who had a dream took the incredibly brave leap to invest in something they believed in but didn't realise how the real world worked until it was too late. I eventually moved away in the end, but finding myself recently in the vicinity I swung by the place. It's now a men's barbershop.

An underlying point I'm trying to make here is that there's a risk in everything you do. There's a risk in crossing the road. There's a risk when you drive to work every day, and you assume no one else will make a mistake on the road.

There's a risk in all types of investing, whether it be stocks, property, or buying a business.

But you greatly exacerbate that risk when you don't know what you're doing.

Investing in stocks without knowing what you are doing could be considered the equivalent of driving to work without having taken any driving lessons before. It's the equivalent of walking into an operating theatre, grabbing a scalpel and just having a go at open heart surgery. It's like having a crack at building the foundations for someone's new home or trying to land a 747 because you saw it on the Krypton Factor once.

The odds are firmly stacked against your success.

And so my opening message to you in this book is as follows.

If you want to invest in stocks successfully, you're going to need someone to walk you through it: a trainer, a coach or a mentor. You cannot successfully fly a plane, build foundations, perform heart surgery or pick the right stocks to invest in without guidance and training.

It will merely end badly otherwise.

As with almost everything these days, there are people in the world that can help you with this. People who have been there and done it and know how to teach it down. People you get on with, like and can enjoy the learning process with.

You do not need to be one of those investors who loses their money due to their stupidity and spends the rest of their days warning others against it.

If you have already lost money in the past because you didn't know any better, then it's time to step up, own your mistakes and say "I messed up".

At which point we can now move forward. There's still time to make some significant returns. Even periods of market crashes are excellent profit opportunities. There is no excuse.

This book has been designed to take you from an amateur investor to a savvy investor. I am going to show you precisely what I have done to achieve the 163% return I have gained over the last five years (32.6% annually) and how anyone can achieve these same results by using a straightforward strategy to invest in stocks.

CHAPTER 4
MY INVESTING PHILOSOPHY

WHY YOU CAN'T PREDICT SHORT TERM MARKETS

It's a scientific fact today that humans are pretty awful at making predictions. Studies have been carried out for years on the inability of us being able to predict the outcome of certain things and to do so consistently over time. Even so, called 'experts' predicting events in their respective fields fail these studies.

Of course, everyone knows someone who got it right once or twice. The laws of probability suggest this would be so even with a low success rate. I mean, you still got 3 picks correct out of the ten you made with a 30% hit rate. It's smaller than 50/50 of course, but it's those three picks that everyone remembers. That's because we 'want' to believe it's possible.

On a surprise trip I took her on my daughter predicted that we were going to a particular restaurant. Aged 7 years old, she was over the moon that her prediction was right. She still won't shut up about how she "knew" she was right all along, and this happened months ago now.

This is a testament to the fact that we feel a certain buzz when we get a call right. It makes us feel powerful and godlike. It's intoxicating even. "Look at me; I got it right!". We are hardwired this way from birth, evidenced by the reaction of an innocent seven-year-old girl.

I think we can all relate to that time we got it right and somewhat childishly wanted everyone to know about it.

But this isn't evidence of any ability to predict with accuracy, nor with consistency, and the studies carried out (you can find these easily on Google) show we are particularly poor at it.

Yet we love predictions. We are attracted to them, and in an industry where we all want an edge, we even crave them.

An analyst can come out with a report of the top three FTSE 250 stocks that will catapult next week, and suddenly our greedy little ears will prick up, and we'll show a keen interest in finding out which stocks they're referring to.

Mystic Meg achieved a primetime TV slot on the National Lottery in the UK for a reason. It wasn't for her accuracy or consistency mind you. Telling the nation that the winner that week would have a red door and the number 7 in their phone number meant the odds were pretty high of getting a few hits in a nation of 65 million people.

She was there because the television network knew the nation loved hearing predictions. Her accuracy and consistency were never considered. People on their sofas watching the colourful balls spin around lapped it up every week. "ooh, Brian, we have a red door, it might be us!".

It's the very reason horoscopes are still even a thing, and tarot card readers always somehow make a living. It's the same reason we're prepared to sit through an hour of Alan Shearer telling us what he thinks will happen today before the big match kicks off.

And so by now, I hope I've made my feelings about stock market predictions abundantly clear to you're the reader.

For every opinion that Gold will go up this week, you will find an equal number of predictions that the price of Gold will fall. How does that help me in any way make a decision? It doesn't.

In my years as a trader and investor, I have never seen any evidence that anyone can predict the outcome of short term markets with accuracy and consistency.

Hang on….short term markets? What are they?

I'm talking about predicting what a price might do in the next minute, the next 5 minutes, the next 10 minutes, the next hour, the next 12 hours or even the next day. Hell, I don't believe anyone can predict what a stock price is going to do in the next week and maybe even the next month. That is my honest and upfront opinion.

I know for sure that I do not have this ability, and anyone who makes predictions for a living must surely feel a pang of imposter syndrome every day of their lives. For they too must know they don't have any unique ability themselves. They are entertainers more than anything. Feeding the crowd what they want to hear, not what they need.

However….(and here is the caveat).

I do believe we can put the odds in our favour.

This is different from predicting a price will go up. Instead, we are saying "this stock has better odds of going up compared to others".

I am, therefore in the business of 'putting the odds in my favour'.

But my power of manipulating the odds is still somewhat limited. I don't believe I can change the odds in the short term. I cannot improve the odds of a share price going up over the next minute, for instance. If you asked me, I would have to say I have no idea what it will do.

If you asked me whether a price is likely to go up over the next week, I'd have no idea. Or the next day. To me, that is impossible to know.

But, I can hand on heart tell you whether the price of a stock is likely or unlikely to rise over the next 1-5 years relative to the other companies that surround it. THAT I can do, and that is the extraordinary power that I bring to you.

How much will it rise by? I can't say. I do not know. But by identifying and investing in the stocks that have the best odds of going up in value, I've achieved some superb results.

How did I accumulate this power? Let me explain.

HOW TO PUT THE ODDS IN YOUR FAVOUR

I have spent many years trying to work out how to pick the right stocks. I tried fundamental analysis (looking at trends in the world and patterns in behaviours), technical analysis (looking at charts and patterns in historical share price) and I spent years coming up short.

Nothing I tried seemed to improve my results much above the results achieved from random selection. In other words, nothing I tried seemed to add any value to my stock selection process. I could have picked blindfolded and done just as well.

For a long time, I became resigned to the idea that there was just no way to pick between the different stocks on offer. I believed the only solution for me as an investor was to pick at random and manage that trade carefully. If it failed, I would get out quick, and it it worked I would stay in. For a long time, this produced decent results.

But eventually, I began to get curious about what drove the share prices up and down. Why did some stocks seem to be doing so well, while others were headed down?

Now, of course, this is primarily driven by market sentiment. In other words, the beliefs of shareholders and investors. It all came down to supply and demand. If lots of investors wanted to buy shares in a company, this would drive prices higher. If no-one were interested in buying shares in a company, then the price would have to fall to find buyers.

The housing market operates similarly. A house is only

going to be sold at a price someone is happy to buy at. If no one wants to buy your home at £325,000, you won't sell it. To sell it, you'll need to lower your price. This is what's happening when share prices are falling. No one is buying. There is more supply than demand.

This led me to ask myself then, "ok, so what drives that sentiment?. What makes an investor want to buy more or buy none?".

The answer to that is incredibly vast and complicated. There are too many strategies, ideas and opinions that surround the markets for anyone to be able to put their finger directly onto it.

However, what I did work out was the first important step to building and designing myself a stock selection criteria that would go on to beat the overall market five years in a row between 2014-2019 and produce an annual return of over 30% a year.

Here's what I discovered.

I found that the financial performance of a company had a reliable correlation to the price of its shares going up and down.

Which makes total sense, right? How else would one judge the performance of a business?

A company is surely deemed to be a roaring success if they are consistently making big profits. A company losing profits or not making any money at all would be considered a failing business whose days were numbered if they continued in that fashion.

But, there was more to it I found. For instance, some of the huge staples of the FTSE 100, for example, were making big profits, but their share price wasn't doing well.

Here were some of the UK's most important household names, with revenues of billions, and yet their share price looked range-bound for many years with no apparent rising trend or rising pattern.

A deeper dive into this led me to my principle set of rules that would later guide me in my stock selection criteria.

You see, it wasn't so much whether they were making a profit as such that seemed to lead to a significant rise in share price, but in fact, how efficient they were.

I was finding tiny FTSE Small Cap companies with revenues of under £200m a year who were more efficient with that money than some of the big global supergiants who had £100 bn revenue a year.

This was fascinating to me. Firstly, it explained why some small companies share prices had been skyrocketing to over 1000% return over the last five years. Secondly, it explained why some of the big global powerhouses who were bringing in way more in revenue had only seen a 5% rise in share price over that same period.

And when it comes to investing my money and getting the most substantial return possible on it, it's these 1000% return companies I wanted to be investing in.

It opened my eyes to the mistakes I had been making for years in picking at random and hoping for the best. Upon crunching the numbers, I began to find that many of the stocks I had previously invested in were complete duds. Companies with big names whose products I liked, but who financially were not achieving much as a business.

I obtained a new fresh excitement for investing in stocks. I was fascinated to test this out.

I spent the next year doing exactly that.

This led to me eventually building my 'criteria'. A mechanical, factual checklist that I could put every stock up against equally to identify the best of the best stocks out there on the markets. Not focused on revenue or size, but on their efficiency relative to their everyday recurring business.

Some companies were making £200m in revenue but keeping 60% of that money as profit. They were growing year on year, and we're doing amazing things with their earnings. Paying more substantial dividends, pumping the money into cash reserves for future acquisitions of competitors and reinvesting much of the profits into purchasing assets for the business to help them increase revenues and therefore increase profits. Some were even buying back their shares from the public to reduce the number out there that existed, driving up demand for them and thus raising their share price even higher.

However, some of the big household name companies (and many of the small unknowns too) were in far worse shape. Some hadn't seen a rise in revenue in the last ten years. Some were posting losing years. Some had increasing debt levels that they would struggle to pay off if they weren't careful. Some had rising expenses year on year, rising faster than the overall revenue coming in each year. Some were profitable but showed a steady trend in declining efficiency.

Many of them were profitable overall. They just weren't as efficient as others. Based on their revenue, they should have been making far more profit. They should have been keeping a larger slice of the 'pie'.

Companies like BP, Tesco, Sainsbury's, Mothercare, Debenhams, Thomas Cook, GlaxoSmithKline, Tate & Lyle and many more were profitable but were keeping the thinnest slice possible from their revenue.

It meant that the slightest hiccup could result in posting a losing year for these businesses. Losing years do not prompt rising share prices, of course.

Not long after looking at Thomas Cook, Mothercare and Debenhams, and dismissing all three of these as companies I wouldn't touch with a barge pole, they closed down. Each was slowly falling off the markets altogether.

I saw it from miles off.

Not because of any ability to predict as such. But purely because the financials showed me the trouble they were each in.

I posted as such in my Facebook group long before the news came out. Again, it wasn't a prediction. I was explaining the odds. The odds were that these companies wouldn't have a very rosy future if they didn't make instant changes to the way they were going.

Each company took me 2-3 hours of analysis. Looking through their financials and analysing the information that was important to me in telling me how efficient the company were performing.

I didn't care about the brand. I had no opinion involved in any of the companies. I just wanted to know who passed my test.

My test was mechanical. A yes or no checklist that meant a company either passed the grade, or it didn't. After

[MTC] Mothercare plc

The first inkling we had that Mothercare plc had issues was back in April 2014, some five years ago. Their latest financial report showed the second year in a row of revenue decline from 2012's £812m, 2013's £749m and then 2014's £724m.

Expenses were also rising back then and in 2014 amounted to 125% of the gross profit. Resulting in a loss before tax and interest. Interest on held debt was growing too, and the company reported a net loss of -£27.5m. Their share price at the time sat at £1.30.

Revenue has fallen every single year since then, with alarming consistency. Expenses have grown astronomically, accounting for 892% of the gross profit in 2018. Huge net losses in 2018 and 2019 sealed their fate, but in truth, the warning signs were there back in 2014.

Mothercare plc failed the criteria miserably and would never have been considered for investment even back in 2008 long before the issues began to surface for them.

Today their share price sits at £0.12p per share.

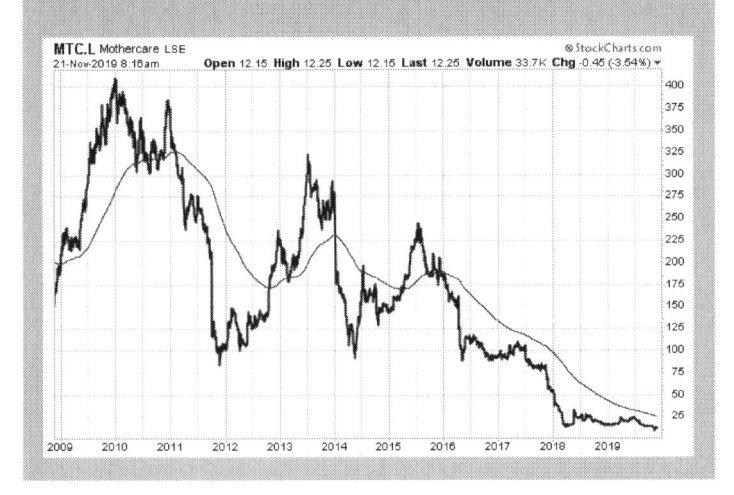

analysing my first 100 companies, many of which came from the FTSE 100 the UK's top 100 stocks, I found only 15 passed my test.

Of course, my next step was to define the criteria for 'when' they passed.

Some companies, for instance, retrospectively failed the test for a few years and then began passing the test each year as they became stronger and more efficient as a business.

It was, therefore, necessary to employ a black/white, hard/fast set of rules that gave no room for opinion or bias. A collection of rules that would tell me the date for when I could definitively confirm that this company would have been added to my watchlist/portfolio.

Once established, I then cross-referenced these dates of entry to the share price at the time. This allowed me to not only measure the performance of each of these stocks since achieving entry to my watchlist but to also put these results up against the performance of the overall FTSE 100. I did this to create a benchmark score that needed to be beaten to know if the process was adding value.

The results achieved are covered at the beginning of this book, and I can hand on heart say they have been fantastic for me and those who have been following me.

This is precisely how I managed to put the odds in my favour.

Remember, no predictions are going on here. I am not predicting that these companies will make you lots of money. I do not have that ability.

The criteria I have built selects stocks that have the highest odds of going up in value over the next 1-5 years based on the facts. Unlike other analysts whose reports I've read, I do not provide any of my own opinions on what I "think" a companies share price will do. Nor do I hold any bias towards any companies that I might "like".

I have realised that such bias adds zero value in the business of stock selection, and I am not in the business of adding anything to my investment decisions that add zero value.

THE NOISE OF THE MARKETS

I was sitting at my barbers one Saturday morning getting the beard fixed up, and while waiting in the chair, I unsociably jumped on my mobile phone. I had received a new message from a well-respected analyst working for a gigantic +100,000 subscriber stock pick newsletter.

"Check out this gravity-defying brand new stock; no one has heard about", read the title of the message.

Now, by this point in my life, I had been reading these long enough to know these "alerts" (as they call them) are simply clickbait posts. They are always too good to be true but are titled in a way to provoke curiosity.

And with +100,000 subscribers, if no one knew about this stock, they certainly did now.

But as a fellow analyst, I'm often a sucker for these click-bait posts. I find myself curious about which stocks these analysts and newsletters are recommending to their clients. I cannot help myself wanting to see how they match up to my self built criteria.

Will this so-called fantastic company they recommend pass my test? Or are they just another mediocre business being pushed by some opinion based analyst? I am always fascinated to know what's being pushed out there.

A SMALL CAP STOCK THAT COULD SMASH THE FTSE 100 THIS YEAR!

"Fast-fashion retailer QUIZ (LSE: QUIZ) has gained 7.6%. At a share price of 170.5p, its market capitalisation is £212m. I reckon this specialist in occasionwear and dressy casualwear has every prospect of continuing to outperform the FTSE 100.

It currently operates 71 stores in the UK and the board believes that there's potential for a further 40 to 50 stores in the medium-to-long term. International expansion represents a significant opportunity, with the company using multiple routes to international markets, including online, as well as standalone stores, concessions, and franchise and wholesale partners.

The price-to-earnings (P/E) ratio is 21.2 and with EPS growth of 24.2%, the price-to-earnings growth (PEG) ratio is 0.88, which is on the good value side of the PEG fair value marker of one. A forecast dividend of 1.73p gives a prospective yield of just over 1%, as the board pursues a progressive dividend policy."

Just for a moment, I want to break this particular stock pick down.

Firstly, it's entirely opinion-based. "I reckon", "has every prospect" and "the board believes" are not factual statements. They are opinion-based statements.

Where are the facts? Where is the factual deduction that led to his decision making?

You can reckon it's going to do great all you want. But I want factual information — evidence to support such a claim.

Secondly, the analyst has clumsily thrown some stats and ratio's into the article in an attempt to impress and bolster the article. But any shrewd, educated analyst knows that on their own these stats mean very little. You certainly couldn't use an EPS ratio or a P/E ratio on their own to deduce whether a stock was a good investment. If only it were that easy……

But I'm fascinated at this point. I know the article is BS. I know there's nothing concrete in here. But as I say, I can't help myself.

So I let the barber do his thing, I spent the day with my family, and in the evening once everyone was winding down for the day, I fired up my laptop, eager to dig further.

I found the financial data and systematically began punching the numbers into the specifically dedicated spreadsheet I have designed to help me identify the information I need.

After an hour or so I needn't carry on. I can already see where it is going. But as a man who hates leaving something like this half-finished, I complete the job.

[QUIZ] Quiz plc

Since floating on the stock market in 2017 with a share price valuation of £1.82 results had been weak. They didn't qualify for the watchlist in 2017 and were quite some way off doing so.

So when results published in April 2018 showed a decline in performance, this would have put them deep into my "check them again in a few years" category.

We would never have invested in a declining business, despite what the analysts were recommending to their subscribers. Regardless of what EPS scores and P/E ratios they were getting excited about.

There was no personal opinion here whatsoever. The financials told us everything we needed to know. We made a decision not to invest based on 100% factual data.

Today the share price sits at £0.17p.

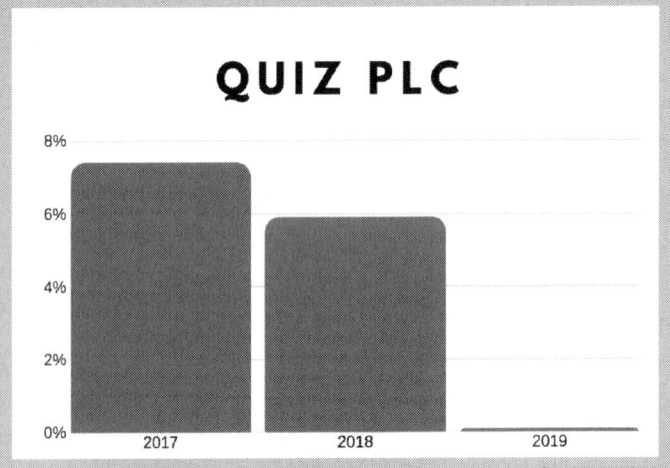

QUIZ PLC

QUIZ plc's declining net profits 2017-2019

Now, I can categorically say that we would never have invested in QUIZ. It's easy for me to say retrospectively I know, but let me back myself up with the facts here.

REVENUE
It's essential to make it clear here that QUIZ plc's revenue had been rising three years in a row. Meaning more and more money had been coming into the business each year. However, as you'll see, this doesn't paint the full picture for us yet.

GROSS MARGIN FALLING
Gross Margin fell from 62.7% to 60.7%. This represents the slice of the profits kept from incoming revenue after cost of the goods they've sold have been taken into account. Not a big deal here, but it's moving in the wrong direction.

RISING EXPENSES
A more significant concern here is the rising expenses. Now we can take a look at the £ figure for the expenses, but that doesn't give us an accurate visual of the issue for a company whose revenue has been rising. We would expect expenses to go up somewhat as the company increases income. Therefore the more useful figure to work from is the % of these expenses relative to the revenue coming in. This shows us that in 2017 their operating expenses (wages, rents, rates, etc.) cost the business 85% of their gross profits. By 2018 this has risen to 88.3%. By 2019 this rose again to 99.7%.

Let me make that 100% clear. The companies expenses were .3% less than all the profit that came in. Meaning QUIZ plc have £200k left from £130 million. And we haven't even removed taxes yet.

NET PROFIT

Looking at the % of profit against what came into the business (i.e. the efficiency of that business) we can see that in 2017 they made a respectable (but not strong enough) 7.4% return. In 2018 this fell to 5.9%. By 2019 this fell to 0.1%.

Looking at the data, I can, therefore, deduce the following;-

QUIZ plc was never a strong enough business to consider buying shares in

Many of the critical financial numbers were falling, not rising

We knew upon the release of their April 2018 financial report that the numbers were headed in the wrong direction.

The alert was sent out by the analyst back in September 2018.

So, either the analyst:-

- knew the results were going south at the time of releasing the alert but didn't care
- didn't think it was important
- didn't even crunch these numbers

This analyst told over 100,000 subscribers indirectly to buy this stock as he felt they were going to beat the FTSE 100.

Want to know the tragic end to this story?

Just four weeks later after the release of the alert, the price tanked from £1.70p a share to just £0.50p a share. From there it has continued it's slide to £0.17p a share.

I daren't try to imagine how many of the 100,000 subscribers poured money into that recommendation.

You would think that with such responsibility, the analyst would have crunched these numbers.

And here's the thing. Maybe he did. Perhaps he knew and didn't care? Maybe what he does has nothing to do with actually making his subscribers any money. His company has already collected its subscription fees, after all.

Or perhaps this analyst only cares about the top-level data? Data which on its own can be very misleading. We have to wonder just how well this analyst does with his own portfolio if he's making picks like these.

I find it commonplace amongst investors to look at the revenue of a business alone when determining whether it is a company with whom they should invest.

I would argue that such an amateur approach to investing is perilous, however. For in the example of QUIZ plc, here is a company posting increasing revenues each year, whose share price has now fallen something like 90% in value in 2 years.

I feel terrible for those who might have lost money following this pick and many others. Yet it must happen all the time — the blind leading the blind.

It also adds more weight and strength to the work I am doing. The fact is, here is a company who's downfall was evident in their finances for all to see if only they'd looked and knew what to look for.

I can accept it if a superbly performing business suddenly with no warning takes a hit and their share price falls.

It's rare (Extremely rare, as the warning signs are usually evident in the financials before it occurs), but I would be more forgiving in that scenario.

But to recommend a company who's financials already show signs of decline, and make out that they are going to be a huge success is downright poor form in my book, and it is the very reason I pursue and run my own analysis.

Debenhams falls into administration, wiping out Mike Ashley's stake

This headline came from a story in 2019 taken from the Guardian newspaper.

It covered the downfall of Debenhams plc, a company of which Sports Direct International owner & investor Mike Ashley held £150 million worth of shares. He'd lost the lot.

Once again, the numbers told us everything, however. While revenues were rising the whole time, expenses were rising significantly quicker year on year. From 48% in 2013 to 73% in 2017. These costs were seemingly out of control. Each year posted worse profits from 2014 onwards. Debenhams never qualified for my criteria. Their results were never strong enough. What's more, the warning signs of trouble were there from 2014 onwards when it was clear expenses were getting out of control.

Strange then that Mike Ashley continued to purchase more shares after 2014, the year the numbers began to show a steady decline. He increased his stake in Debenhams each year despite the companies consistently failing financial results.

YEAR	SHARES HELD	STAKE
2012	0	0%
2013	0	0%
2014	56m	4.6%
2015	128m	10.5%
2016	128m	10.5%
2017	142m	11.5%
2018	364m	29.7%

Either they didn't care about the financial warnings, they didn't realise what they meant, or they didn't even look. Evidence that even the so-called professionals have no idea what they're doing.

KEEPING THINGS SIMPLE

I consider myself an ambassador of keeping things simple and staying away from over-complication. Especially when it comes to trading and investing.

I do not know if this is a reflection of my lack of brainpower or not, but the fact remains that more straightforward approaches often work far better than complicated strategies when it comes to the stock market.

The stock market is an industry rife with analysts and experts trying to flog you their latest algorithms, robots, secret code that beats the markets 99.9% of the time and will guarantee riches.

Only for the end-user to find that after a few months of trying to use it, it hasn't helped them. They'll often be told that "you didn't implement it properly" if they get any feedback at all following a complaint.

I know because I get between 1-2 emails a week from traders and investors who have been deceived or lured into the marketing to part with hellishly expensive levels of cash for what is essentially a pointless piece of software which adds no value.

"I bought this software for £2000, and I have saved up to buy six screens now set up at my trading desk, and I subscribe to this £500/m newsletter, but I'm still not making any profit."

Imagine their dismay then when I explain to them that all I use to make over 30% a year (on average over the last five years) is a laptop, my broker platform and the free charts you can view on the internet.

You don't even need a powerful computer to run any of it. As long as you have an internet connection, you're good to go.

Yet human beings have a bias towards complication. We often assume that complicated = better. In my experience, the opposite is the case. The more involved you make things, the more damage you cause. You can damage a perfectly profitable trading system or strategy by adding further layers of complication to it.

I often get clients come to me telling me "I know this isn't part of the strategy, but would it be okay if I started trading x, y and z?" or "I know this is against what you say, but could I add x,y,z indicator to my entry and exit rules?".

Hey, look. It's their money. I can't be worrying about things I can't control. If they want to piss their money up the wall by adding more layers, who am I to stop them?

Perhaps 163% over the last five years is not good enough. They want more.

Fine, I can assure them that adding more layers to the strategy won't be the way to get there.

But it's so common that I've come to realise that it's deeply ingrained within us. We seem compelled to want to tweak and tinker to make things better.

This psychological bias probably lends itself well to inventors and those working in the technology and science industries. But it tends to sabotage results in the stock market.

That's my experience anyhow.

And the truth is, investing in the stock market needn't be complicated. It is incredibly simple.

Don't get me wrong here. It's not always easy. The psychological rollercoaster of having your money growing and reducing in value every day can take its toll on some people for sure. But this doesn't detract from the fact that when it's all boiled down, it's an incredibly simple process.

- Deposit capital to a broker account
- Identify the right companies to invest in
- Buy shares in those companies
- Buy more shares every month as and when you can
- Re-invest the dividends to buy more even shares
- Sell your shares if the company is no longer the right company to invest in

Of course, questions such as which broker to use, how to pick the stocks and how much to buy of each company are the nuances of a strategy that I'll be helping you with throughout this book.

But overall, this is the basic routine you need to follow.

No expensive hardware or software. No complicated indicators or rules. No specialist equipment.

All you need is a laptop, an internet connection, a broker account and some training/education.

CHAPTER 5
WHY INVEST?

ASSETS & LIABILITIES

To truly understand why you should invest, you need to understand what ASSETS and LIABILITIES are. You also need to know why you want assets and why you don't want liabilities.

You may already understand this simple concept. Yet many don't, and therefore I would be grossly remiss to leave it out of this book.

For me, building my portfolio of assets is one of the most exciting aspects of investing. With every asset I purchase, I grow my wealth.

Every book you'll read on building and growing wealth will tell you that you need to do one thing. One fundamental rule that if followed correctly, will bring you more money in your lifetime.

This rule I'm referring to is the accumulation of assets.

There are two straightforward, yet significant differences between assets and liabilities.

ASSETS put money INTO your pocket. LIABILITIES take money OUT of your pocket.

For example. Let's say you have £2000. Now there are a million different things on which you could spend that money. Some of these things would be classed as assets; some would be classed as liabilities. The way you tell the difference is based on whether they bring money in for you, or take money away.

A new TV, for example, is a liability. You might enjoy getting the latest top of the range screen that's bigger than anything else in your room. You might thoroughly enjoy showing it off to your friends when they come round to watch the football one night. And damn, doesn't Star Wars look so much better in 3D or 4K etc.

But, does a TV bring you any money in? Not usually. It's generally going to take money out of your pocket. You'll get nothing back.

Cars are some of the worst investments you can ever make. Where else can you buy something, drive it home and already lose 30% of the value on it just because it now has had its first owner?

But cars go beyond that. If the drop in core value doesn't scare you, think of the money that comes out of your pocket every month for the finance payments, the road tax, the yearly mot, the fuel you have to buy to keep it running and the repairs when things go wrong.

This is all money going out with nothing coming in. Cars are a liability, much as a TV would be.

So what are assets?

Assets are things you can buy and own which bring money to your pockets.

Some examples of assets could be:-

YOUR OWN START-UP BUSINESS

If you have started a business and it makes you a profit then that business is an asset of yours. It's something you've created that's putting money into your pocket. If however, the business is losing you money, it's a liability.

PROPERTY

If you own property that you can rent out or sell for a profit, then it's an asset that you own. However, if you live in your house, it is not an asset. It is a liability as it is not generating any income for you.

BUYING A BUSINESS

If you were to buy the local chip shop in town for £100,000 and become its new owner, it might well be an excellent asset for you providing it made you a profit after costs and debts. If of course, the company costs were so high that it took money from you, it would be a liability.

SHARES IN OTHER BUSINESSES

Alternatively, you could buy a slice of a public limited company. A 'plc' sells shares in its business to raise capital and has a board in place to determine what to do with that money. These shares can rise and fall in value on the stock market.

Most plc's also issue dividends to shareholders. The amount you are paid is based on the amount the company decides to pay out, divided by the number of shares you own at the time from all the shares in circulation.

Buying shares in businesses that are already established and doing amazingly well is a great way to invest. Especially in comparison to the others which are all relatively time-consuming and bring with them huge risks such as tenants not paying rents and start-up businesses failing to make a profit).

Buying shares allows you to ride the success of other people arguably more skilled than you at running their businesses.

Identify a great company that is already doing everything right and purchase your slice of it. These days all you have to do is open a brokerage account and click your mouse a few times.

A share in a company is an asset in 2 ways: capital gains and dividends.

If you today bought shares in a company with £2000, that stock value can go up. It can do so the very next day, or over a year. But in doing so, you can sell that share for a profit. Hence why it is money coming into your pocket.

However, where things get extra exciting is in the dividends. You see, companies that sell shares also like to reward their shareholders by paying out a bonus, otherwise known as a 'dividend', to its shareholders. This is usually a reward to say thanks for investing, as well as an incentive to attract new investors.

Dividends come in all shapes and sizes with different companies paying different amounts and at different times. Some companies pay big dividends relative to their share price (high yield), and others pay small amounts (low yield). You will also find that some companies pay these dividends monthly, quarterly, half-yearly or yearly.

These dividends are paid into your trading account.

BUY YOUR STOCKS LIKE YOU BUY YOUR GROCERIES

I love spending my money on assets. Every single month I buy more shares in the companies that I've identified as the best companies to invest within. Usually, my focus is more on capital gains than on the dividend yield. But both factors are a consideration when selecting shares to buy.

Just as I buy my food and toothpaste every month, my shopping list also includes "shares".

There is nothing better than the feeling of adding assets to my ever-growing portfolio. A portfolio of assets which each bring in a little more income for me every time I add more to it both via capital gains and dividends.

I reinvest my dividends to buy new stocks each month. This allows me to buy more shares with my money, making more dividends back in the future. It's a prime example of compounded interest at work.

For me, it's a no brainer. Own a flashy TV that will lose me money that I'll never see again, or own shares in a company all set to do well over the next 2-5 years and watch my money grow as a result.

One day you may even be able to reach the point where the income from your shares outweighs the expenditure of your liabilities. At this point, you are classed as financially free, as you would no longer need to gain an income from work.

UNDERSTANDING DIVIDENDS

When you purchase shares in a company, you own a slice of that business. It may well be a very thin slice, but a slice nonetheless.

To reward existing investors and attract new ones, most public limited companies will pay a dividend. A dividend is essentially a chunk of the profits that business had made, split up by the number of shares currently held by investors, and paid out to them.

The more shares you own, the more of that profit you'll be paid.

Remember, when we talk about profits we are talking about what's left after all costs have been considered. The business operating costs, staff wages and director bonuses etc. have already been extracted by this point.

It's like having a load of money left and thinking "what the hell do we do with this extra cash?".

That's where the board come in. Their job is to work out how to use that surplus profit each year to grow the business for its shareholders (i.e. you). If they do it well, the company grows and the share price increases. If they do it poorly, or circumstances outside of their hands occurs, the opposite can happen.

How the board invests that profit is a critical consideration for me in my analysis of a business.

There are a few options available to the board. Here's a couple of common ones:-

RESERVES
They can pump some of the profit into a pot (cash reserves) to be used at a later time. This might be to take-over another company, preferably one that complements the existing business, or to acquire one of their competitors, giving the business more dominance in their industry. Or it may be used for a rainy day to ensure the company continue to stay solvent and grow.

DIVIDENDS
They can use some of the profit to pay a dividend to its shareholders. Rewarding them for being a shareholder and ultimately attracting new investors looking for a robust, reliable dividend payout.

ASSETS
They can use some of the profit to purchase more income-producing assets for the business to aid in growth and increase profitability for the future. These assets could be property, plant, equipment or intangible assets such as rights, patents or trademarks, for instance.

Some companies pay dividends once per year, others half-yearly. Some even pay quarterly and monthly. Often however these more frequent payout schedules are lower in value, so they balance out despite the change in frequency of payouts.

UNDERSTANDING EX-DIVIDEND DATES

To qualify for a dividend payout, you have to own shares in a company before the EX-DIVIDEND date. This is essentially the cut off period. Anyone who purchases shares after this date will have to wait until the next dividend payout to get anything.

It is like a snapshot of who owns shares on this date.

If you buy 100 shares in SGE Sage Group plc on 10th November and the ex-div date is 11th November, then you'll qualify for the upcoming payout, which is often around a week or two after the ex-div date.

If you bought on the 12th however, then you'll have missed out on the upcoming payout and will have to wait until the next announced payout.

When deciding which stocks to invest in each month for your portfolio, awareness of that companies ex-dividend date can be useful to know. It may help you choose where to pump your funds first so that you qualify for the upcoming dividend payout.

UNDERSTANDING DIVIDEND YIELD

The amount of profit each company puts into paying dividends to its investors differs significantly between businesses and largely depends on the companies recent performance. (Some companies will commit to certain levels of dividends despite the performance, which has its pros and cons).

The amount of shares in circulation also differs significantly between companies, of course.

We must also bear in mind that the share price of a company is continuously fluctuating almost minute by minute, day by day.

Therefore if you want to know what return you are getting on the shares you've purchased, it can be tricky to identify.

Ultimately, however, the underlying calculation is to work out what dividend amount you are being paid per share and divide that by what you paid for the shares you own (share price).

This is, of course, something you'll have to work out for yourself.

How much am I getting? / How much did I pay?

However, in the industry, one way of roughly measuring the strength of a dividend payout is the DIVIDEND YIELD.

The Dividend Yield is a measure which takes the dividend payout per share (often confirmed by the company themselves) and then divides this by the share price at the time. This can give you a rough idea of the strength of a dividend.

$$\frac{\text{DIVIDEND PAYOUT}}{\text{SHARE PRICE}} = \text{DIVIDEND YIELD}$$

Some companies have a very generous dividend payout. Others, not so much.

Looking at 27 companies from the CLEAN Watchlist at the time of publishing, the dividends are what I would describe as 'average'.

#	Yield	#	Yield
		14	1.11%
1	2.33%	15	1.87%
2	0.79%	16	4.67%
3	3.13%	17	2.43%
4	4.55%	18	3.60%
5	1.57%	19	1.69%
6	2.04%	20	1.01%
7	2.72%	21	0.69%
8	2.09%	22	0.13%
9	6.88%	23	2.55%
10	2.94%	24	1.48%
11	3.14%	25	4.27%
12	1.59%	26	2.02%
13	1.74%	27	1.18%

This however is just a snapshot taken on a certain date and time. If you buy the stocks at cheaper prices then your yield on those stocks will probably be greater.

CONCERNS WITH DIVIDEND INVESTING

Some investors pick their stocks purely based on the dividend. I have seen many investment coaches who sell courses on dividend investing. They try and find the stocks with the greatest dividend yield %, often companies which payout monthly, and they invest in them solely for that reason.

However, the downside to this approach is that a company pumping higher than average levels of profit into their dividend payouts are unable to re-invest that capital into the business to stimulate growth.

If they are pumping a significant % of yearly profits into attractive dividends, then this is less capital available to put into reserves, used for mergers and acquisitions or used to purchase income-producing assets.

It shows a focus on the now, as opposed to a slow a steady growth.

As a result, it's not often that you'll find a high dividend yield stock achieving a stable share price growth.

Equally, reliable companies whose share prices are growing, often do not have super impressive dividend yields.

How you choose to invest and pick your stocks is entirely up to you the investor.

However, to be clear, my focus is on share price growth and company performance. The dividend is an aside. It has no bearing on my stock selection criteria.

As you'd expect, some of the companies picked by my criteria have high dividend yields, but many do not. In fact, at the time of publishing, the average dividend yield across all of the stocks in the portfolio came to 2.38%.

This means that in theory, if you held an equal value of stock in each of the 27 companies, you could expect to receive around 2.38% of your invested capital in dividend payments over 12 months.

It's not exciting. But the dividends are not the aim here for me. My dividends are immediately reinvested into purchasing more shares in my stock picks, resulting in more returns.

I would much prefer to buy a 1000 shares at £5.00 a share (£5000) and watch them grow to £25.00 a share (£25000) over say 2-5 years. 2.38% of whatever I gain from dividends helps me purchase more shares the next year.

To me, dividends are a bonus. An aside. But they are not the focus and have zero bearings on my criteria's picks.

COMPOUNDED INTEREST

In this section of the book I want to show you the power of re-investment.

By re-investing I am simply referring to the process of taking profits and re-investing them.

- BUY £10000 in SHARES
- RECEIVE £300 in DIVIDENDS
- SPEND £300 in DIVIDENDS to BUY £300 more SHARES
- RECEIVE £305 more in DIVIDENDS
- SPEND £305 more in DIVIDENDS to BUY £305 more in SHARES
- RECEIVE £320 in DIVIDENDS

Below is a table I have created to help you the reader visualise the power of compounding your profits into more profits. For the following table to be possible I have had to make a few assumptions listed here.

- We are staring with a £10,000 principle
- We are adding an additional £2500 to the investment account per year (£208/m)
- Dividends earned at 2.5% are re-invested the following year into buying more shares.
- Returns per year are factored in at an average +20% a year (less than I've been achieving using the watchlist)
- No money will be withdrawn from the account

YR	START BALANCE	YR ADD	DIVIDENDS	TOTAL	20% RETURN	END BALANCE
1	£ 10,000.00	£ -	£ 250.00	£ 10,250.00	£ 2,050.00	£ 12,050.00
2	£ 12,050.00	£ 2,500.00	£ 301.25	£ 14,851.25	£ 2,970.25	£ 15,020.25
3	£ 15,020.25	£ 2,500.00	£ 375.51	£ 17,895.76	£ 3,579.15	£ 18,599.40
4	£ 18,599.40	£ 2,500.00	£ 464.99	£ 21,564.39	£ 4,312.88	£ 22,912.28
5	£ 22,912.28	£ 2,500.00	£ 572.81	£ 25,985.09	£ 5,197.02	£ 28,109.30
6	£ 28,109.30	£ 2,500.00	£ 702.73	£ 31,312.03	£ 6,262.41	£ 34,371.70
7	£ 34,371.70	£ 2,500.00	£ 859.29	£ 37,730.99	£ 7,546.20	£ 41,917.90
8	£ 41,917.90	£ 2,500.00	£ 1,047.95	£ 45,465.85	£ 9,093.17	£ 51,011.07
9	£ 51,011.07	£ 2,500.00	£ 1,275.28	£ 54,786.35	£ 10,957.27	£ 61,968.34
10	£ 61,968.34	£ 2,500.00	£ 1,549.21	£ 66,017.55	£ 13,203.51	£ 75,171.85
11	£ 75,171.85	£ 2,500.00	£ 1,879.30	£ 79,551.14	£ 15,910.23	£ 91,082.08
12	£ 91,082.08	£ 2,500.00	£ 2,277.05	£ 95,859.13	£ 19,171.83	£ 110,253.90
13	£ 110,253.90	£ 2,500.00	£ 2,756.35	£ 115,510.25	£ 23,102.05	£ 133,355.95
14	£ 133,355.95	£ 2,500.00	£ 3,333.90	£ 139,189.85	£ 27,837.97	£ 161,193.92
15	£ 161,193.92	£ 2,500.00	£ 4,029.85	£ 167,723.77	£ 33,544.75	£ 194,738.68
16	£ 194,738.68	£ 2,500.00	£ 4,868.47	£ 202,107.14	£ 40,421.43	£ 235,160.11
17	£ 235,160.11	£ 2,500.00	£ 5,879.00	£ 243,539.11	£ 48,707.82	£ 283,867.93
18	£ 283,867.93	£ 2,500.00	£ 7,096.70	£ 293,464.63	£ 58,692.93	£ 342,560.85
19	£ 342,560.85	£ 2,500.00	£ 8,564.02	£ 353,624.87	£ 70,724.97	£ 413,285.83
20	£ 413,285.83	£ 2,500.00	£ 10,332.15	£ 426,117.97	£ 85,223.59	£ 498,509.42
21	£ 498,509.42	£ 2,500.00	£ 12,462.74	£ 513,472.16	£ 102,694.43	£ 601,203.85
22	£ 601,203.85	£ 2,500.00	£ 15,030.10	£ 618,733.95	£ 123,746.79	£ 724,950.64
23	£ 724,950.64	£ 2,500.00	£ 18,123.77	£ 745,574.41	£ 149,114.88	£ 874,065.53
24	£ 874,065.53	£ 2,500.00	£ 21,851.64	£ 898,417.17	£ 179,683.43	£ 1,053,748.96
25	£ 1,053,748.96	£ 2,500.00	£ 26,343.72	£1,082,592.68	£ 216,518.54	£ 1,270,267.50
26	£ 1,270,267.50	£ 2,500.00	£ 31,756.69	£1,304,524.18	£ 260,904.84	£ 1,531,172.33
27	£ 1,531,172.33	£ 2,500.00	£ 38,279.31	£1,571,951.64	£ 314,390.33	£ 1,845,562.66
28	£ 1,845,562.66	£ 2,500.00	£ 46,139.07	£1,894,201.73	£ 378,840.35	£ 2,224,403.01
29	£ 2,224,403.01	£ 2,500.00	£ 55,610.08	£2,282,513.08	£ 456,502.62	£ 2,680,905.62
30	£ 2,680,905.62	£ 2,500.00	£ 67,022.64	£2,750,428.26	£ 550,085.65	£ 3,230,991.28

As you can see, with a starting figure of £10,000 this can reach £28,109 by the end of year 5. Assuming dividends made are all reinvested into more stocks each year and not spent then by year 10, this account could be up to £75,171.

Again, by the end of year 15, this would see the account up to £194,738 and after 20 years the principle £10,000 plus the further investment of £47,500 (£2500 a year for 20 years) would be worth just shy of half a million.

By the end of the 20 years, you would have a passive income stream of £10,332 in dividends every year that if spent each year from that point onwards, wouldn't affect your principle £498,509.

Of course, each year onwards the amount becomes super exciting. If you were to pass on the mantle to your kids to continue to grow the account, in just 10 more years the fund would stand at £3.2 million, with £67,022 a year in dividends. Or £5585/m gross.

That's in 30 years.

I'm 37. By 67 years old, I could well be a multi-millionaire.

I certainly intend to be.

But look what happens if we shift the numbers around a bit.

Let's say we start with £15,000 and can afford £3000 further input a year (£250/m)

By the end of the same 30 years, the account would be up to £4.6m with a yearly dividend payment of £97,164 or £8097/m gross.

Of course, we still have room to raise the yearly average. The portfolio so far has achieved 32.6% average return a year, but who's to say that won't drop as an average return over the next 20-30 years? It's impossible to say. It might even rise.

However, these numbers have been crunched with 20% return a year, which is a reasonable expectation in my opinion.

Now, I don't want people to take me too literally. There are so many variables around the returns you'll receive, the yearly injection of further capital and the dividend % that it's impossible to say where the fund will be in 20-30 years.

All this is here to do is to provide you with a visual representation of the power of compounding your profits.

Re-investing your profits for more significant gains in the future.

The more years you take your dividends and re-invest them, the more stocks you can buy. The more shares you can purchase the more dividends you'll recieve. The more dividends you'll get the more stocks you can buy. You're playing with the house money. Money making more money.

It is a money-making machine, and you can build it today, from your laptop. No need to purchase land and property. No need to find the right tenants. No need to find the right manager to run your business or find ways to increase profits.

You can instead find already succeeding businesses, some of the most well-run companies in the UK in fact, and buy your very own slice of them.

CHAPTER 6
ANALYSIS OF A FTSE COMPANY

BUILDING THE CRITERIA

I spent seven years mastering the strategy of knowing when to get in and out of a stock. I used a system which produced entry and exit signals which I followed. This removed all emotional decision making for me — a systematic mechanical approach.

The strategy was simple.

- Define your risk per trade before you start (1% of your capital is healthy)
- Never exceed or lower this risk on any one trade. All trades must be equal in risk.
- Trade every signal (we had no idea which signals would work and which would win, so we had to take every single one with the same level of risk applied).
- Those that failed would generate exit signals soon afterwards, and we would get out before it cost us much capital.
- Those that succeeded would be left alone to continue until an exit signal one day appeared.
- Using this approach, we only needed to be right 30% of the time to be profitable. (10 trades, 3 wins @ £200 each, 7 losses at £40 each = £320 profit).

However, despite making reliable profits using this approach, there was always one big question that bounced around in my head — a question for which I NEEDED to know the answer.

The answer eluded me for a long time.

"How do I know which stocks to pick?".

For a long time, my approach was akin to wearing a blindfold and playing 'pin the tail on the donkey'. While my strategy of keeping losses small and letting winners run worked, I lost big chunks of my potential profit by making bad picks. Companies I would buy would fail soon afterwards. Never costing me much, but slowly adding up over the year.

Later down the line, my approach evolved into picking big companies and businesses with which I was familiar. I traded BP, Vodaphone, Travis Perkins, Debenhams, Dixons, Tate & Lyle and hundreds more UK based stocks that I took on purely based on name alone.

I got burned this way as well. I learned the hard lesson that a name and reputation means very little on what a share price is going to do and where it was going to move.

I continued to focus on refining my stock selection criteria and soon afterwards developed a four filter process.

Applying four filters, I was able to reduce the list of available stocks that met my threshold.

LIQUIDITY

The companies I picked had to have high volume. I didn't want illiquid stocks that weren't being bought and sold regularly by investors. Otherwise, this could lead to sudden drops in share price when shareholders wanted to sell but couldn't find buyers.

MARKET SIZE

They had to have a share price of under £15.00 a share due to my account size.

CORRELATION

I could only have one stock from one sector. Otherwise, I could be trading correlated stocks that moved in sync with each other, ultimately adding more risk to one outcome.

TREND

I would only pick stocks that seemed to be trending upwards, although I found it very difficult to define precisely how to do that.

These four filters helped somewhat to concentrate the vast pool of stocks available to me, but it still wasn't sophisticated enough. I still had stocks blowing out a tyre on the road and costing me money.

I often wondered if it were possible to refine further? Perhaps a ceiling exists in this industry where you cannot improve the odds of your stock picking. The thought did cross my mind. Yet deep down, I knew that my process wasn't as secure as it could be, so I kept learning and studying.

I asked myself "what is the driver for stock prices moving? What causes them to shift?"

The answer I eventually learned was perception. The perception of millions of investors and traders around the world. Specifically, the perception of that stocks value today. This I discovered was primarily based on the financial performance of that business, which made complete sense to me.

So, I began learning how to read financial statements. I studied these financial statements. My background in statistics and accounting were helping significantly here.

I learned how to read the underlying numbers and how to identify what was happening behind the scenes. I learned how to push past the big numbers most investors were swooning at and found the real picture of what was happening, behind the scenes.

In doing so, I built my criteria. Much in keeping with my background in keeping trading mechanical and emotion-free, I designed a hard and fast set of mechanical rules that a company's financials must meet to qualify for the watchlist.

I didn't want any personal opinion to creep into this process. I knew it wouldn't add any value. I wanted facts. Do they, or don't they meet the criteria? No grey areas.

WHAT I'M LOOKING FOR

I was actively looking for the best of the best. I wanted to know the best companies of the FTSE 100, 250, Small Cap, Fledgling and AIM indexes. Which companies were performing the strongest above all others?

Which companies met my very high standards?

The answer was "not many". In fact, of the FTSE 100, only 15 passed the test. In other words, 85 of the UK's Top 100 companies, did not qualify for my watchlist criteria. Their financials were not strong enough for various reasons.

Many were carrying too much debt relative to their earnings ability. Others had expense ratios eating up over 90% of their gross profits. Some companies were making billions, yet only just about turning a profit each year. Others had losing years and looked in awful shape.

But it wasn't all bad. Some of these companies just weren't as good as their neighbours. When you are sifting through a list of 100 companies, and only picking 15 of them, there's a significant number in there that are perfectly profitable and respectable businesses. They just weren't as strong as the 15 that qualified.

You see, I was only after the best of the best. The companies that were smashing it financially and were doing everything right with the profits. I wanted to give myself the greatest odds of picking stocks whose share prices would be valued higher over the next 2-5 years.

I found that these companies had a correlation between their fantastic financials and strong share price growth.

Now I want to make it clear here that I'm not saying these 15 stocks are the only stocks whose share price will rise. I have no idea about that. I'm sure that some of the 85 who failed the test may well increase in value.

What I am instead doing here is putting the odds as much in my favour as possible. By only investing my money into the stocks that stand out as the best financially run, most efficient businesses, I am raising the odds of my portfolio beating the overall market.

It is almost a no brainer that by cherry-picking the best 15 from the FTSE 100, you are dramatically improving the odds of seeing higher returns. Following significant testing, that's precisely what I've been seeing, having beaten the market (FTSE 100) significantly for five years in a row now.

In 2017 the FTSE 100 achieved an increase of 8% in growth across its 100 companies. However, by cherry-picking the best of the best stocks from across the FTSE 100, 250, Small Cap, Fledgling and AIM markets, my portfolio achieved a 38% return over the same period.

In 2018, a losing year, the FTSE 100 dropped in value by -12%. My portfolio also fell in value, but only by -8%.

In 2019 the FTSE rose in value by 10%. My portfolio rose by 29% (at time of publishing).

My portfolio of stocks, identified and picked by my criteria, outperformed the FTSE 100 for five years in a row, and that's what selecting the best and cutting away the deadwood can do for your results.

But what exactly am I looking for in these companies? What allows them to qualify?

REVENUE

A sheer giant of the FTSE 100, BP plc reported yearly revenue of £298 billion in 2019. An astounding figure, rarely seen anywhere else across the FTSE 100. But a high revenue does not necessarily relate to an excellent investment.

BP plc spent £229 billion in cost of sales, £39 billion in operating expenses, £16 billion in depreciation costs, £2.6 billion paying off just the interest on debt alone and had a tax bill of £7.1 billion to pay.

They were left with £4.6 billion. Just 1.5% of the revenue that came in.

Now don't get me wrong. £4.6 billion earnings a year is a figure most companies could only dream about achieving.

But remember here that its all about the perception of value. What I discovered is it's not the revenue nor the raw £ value of what is kept that necessarily leads to the price of a companies shares rising. Some of the highest share price growth has come from small FTSE 250 companies with revenues of under £400 million a year.

What I found was that the odds are very much against BP's shares, doubling in value over the next couple of years. Why? Because they only keep 1.5% of what comes in. The year before that they lost -0.4% (a financial loss of £906 million). The year before that (2017) they lost £3.4 billion.

Revenue can be a massive red herring. Investors flock to it as a guide to success, but as I've often told the women in my life, it's not how big it is that matters, but what you do with it that counts.

[BP.] BP plc

On 15th October 1999, BP's shares were valued at £5.47 at the close of trading. 20 years later, on the 15th October 2019, those shares were worth £4.90.

There has been no sustained share price growth in this business for 20 years, and rightly so when they are losing money one year, and only keeping 1.5% of their revenue the next.

This volatile rollercoaster of a share price is not what i'm interested in. I also have little interest in owning shares in a business that 20 years later are worth less than I bought them for.

Yet BP plc are one of the most popular FTSE 100 stocks to own by investors. The very idea of investing in a oil company feels like a good investment to many people.

This is precisely why I wanted to build a criteria that takes emotions, feelings and brand loyalty out of the equation. It is fascinating under scrutiny just how many of the large brand names fail the test. I relish looking at these big brand company reports today and realising how fortunate I am to have dodged a bullet.

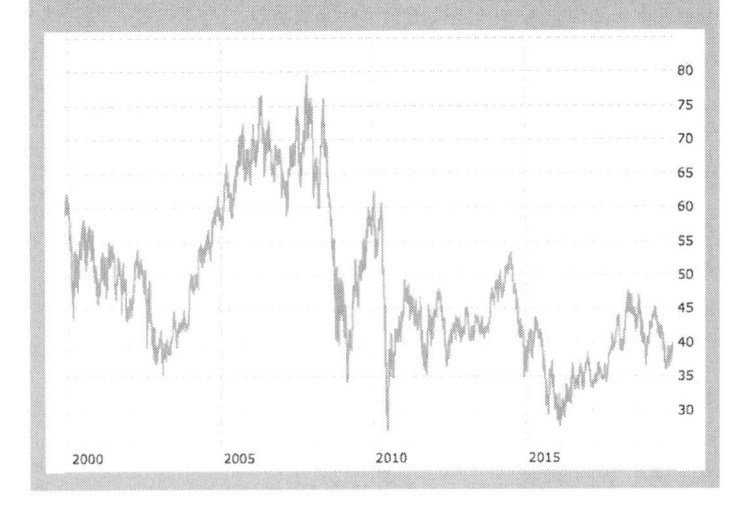

BP plc are miles away from ever qualifying for my watchlist. Looking at the numbers, I doubt it will ever happen. Strong they might be. Mighty, yes, of course. But highly inefficient, and inconsistent. All these financials are also reflected in their share price.

On 15th October 1999, BP's shares were valued at £5.47 at the close of trading. Twenty years later, on the 15th October 2019, those shares were worth £4.90.

There has been no sustained share price growth in this business for 20 years, and rightly so when they are losing money one year, and only making 1.5% of revenue the next.

Compare this to a company such as AB Dynamics plc, who in September 2014 were added to the watchlist after passing my tests. This company had a yearly revenue of £13.8 million, and their share price sat at £1.66.

By September 2019, just five years later, their share price sat at £27.40. And they still only had revenue of £37 million a year by this point.

For me, revenue serves as an indicator that there is business to be won in their industry. It is a measure of the potential only. It is the amount of water entering the filter. The more that comes in, hopefully, the more that will stay after deductions. But this is not always the case. Remember, BP made £240 billion in 2017 and ended up making a loss of -£906 million after costs.

I want to see rising revenue. This indicates growth and business to be won in their industry. It shows me they are in the right place to benefit. Much like a coffee shop being placed in a high traffic zone, rather than down a dark back alley that no one passes. But remember that alone it doesn't tell us much, other than this company has a chance.

Of course, revenue can also be used to identify underlying problems.

Falling revenue is often a real concern, and this alone can cause a company to fail my criteria immediately. A consistent drop in revenue shows an underlying decline in the marketplace and may even be a significant problem outside of the businesses control.

Mothercare plc has been a prime example of this. This table below shows the companies revenues throughout 2012 - 2019.

| 2012: £812m |
| 2013: £749m |
| 2014: £724m |
| 2015: £713m |
| 2016: £682m |
| 2017: £667m |
| 2018: £580m |
| 2019: £513m |

To me, this shows a distinct and obvious trend in the loss of business coming through the doors. It is evidence of a shift in consumer spending habits, and it shows me that fewer and fewer people are buying baby products via Mothercare.

I have my theories as to why. The dominance of Amazon and their next day delivery cannot be competed with. Indeed, on a recent visit to Mothercare a year ago with the wife following the birth of my son I witnessed in their store what I would only describe as a ghost town, full of overpriced products that could easily be bought at 50% of the cost on eBay or Amazon. We were the only customers in this megastore of overpriced goods.

But my opinion plays no part in this. The numbers will always tell me everything I need to know.

Rising revenue represents growth in the industry and growth potential in the business. Falling revenue shows the opposite and is enough for me to immediately stop running any further analysis on a company.

However, rising revenue alone can be misleading. I would certainly never make any investment decisions on this factor without more knowledge.

GROSS PROFIT

When you take the revenue and then deduct the cost of goods or services from it, you are left with the gross profit.

Gross profit represents the slice the business gets to keep before expenses, interest and taxes.

For me, a bigger that slice the better. The thinner that slice is, the more problems that business is going to have staying profitable, achieving growth and ultimately being efficient.

Mothercare plc is once again a perfect example of this. In 2019 they kept hold of just 3.6% of their incoming revenue after cost of goods. In other words, of the £513m revenue that came through the doors, Mothercare only kept a 3.6% slice of it, before expenses, interest on debts and taxes.

3.6% is not a good start, and a low gross profit is a big warning sign of a problem. Especially when we know we have quite a few more costs to come out of that before we reach the bottom line.

EXPENSES

It is here that many companies pass or fail. Most of them fail.

Advertising costs, marketing, staff wages, bonuses, rents, rates and utilities all come under the umbrella of expenses. They often represent the most considerable degree of outgoings within a business.

Some companies have to spend a lot of money to operate their business and bring in the revenue they achieve.

These expenses can sometimes even outweigh the income, resulting in a net loss for the year. Others can run at just 25% of the gross profit. It is a mixed bag.

However, high expenses can take a company with a healthy gross profit, and beat them down into submission. It can destroy a companies ability to be efficient with the revenue coming in.

I see many companies operating with far too high expenses, often leaving them with very little profit by the end of the year. To qualify for the watchlist criteria, a company must have substantial control over their expenses.

RESEARCH & DEVELOPMENT

I try to avoid investing in any companies that have to pump a significant % of their profits into R&D. These are often tech companies or pharmaceutical companies. The £'s amount isn't of particular importance to me. I'm only really interested in understanding the amount relative to their profits.

In other words, what % of profits made by the business are being eaten up by research and development costs? If it's a high percentage, they don't make the grade.

Any company that has to spend a significant % of their profits on R&D is in a highly competitive industry and will struggle to achieve the stand out numbers I'm looking for. Usually, in my experience, there are far better options out there for me to invest my capital with better odds of share price growth.

DEPRECIATION & AMORTISATION

Property depreciates. Vehicles depreciate. Plant and equipment depreciate. The more a company relies on these assets, the more money they must put aside each year to repair and replace them.

Any company with high depreciation costs are putting too much emphasis on property plant and equipment. This can lead to poor years when depreciation costs go up. Poor years can lead to investor concern and a sudden lack of demand for the companies shares, driving prices down.

As an investor, I'm looking to invest in share prices that are rising. As a result, I avoid companies with high depreciation costs relative to their revenue.

INTEREST ON DEBT/FINANCE

Again, what's important here isn't the amount of the interest being paid in a financial sense, but it's relativity to what the company is bringing in. £4 million interest on the debt is a mote of dust on one companies income statement but could represent 50% of another companies profits.

I pay special attention to this as it is the first of a couple of indicators that will confirm whether the company are borrowing too much debt relative to the size of their business and their ability to pay it off.

I've seen several companies allow their debts to get out of hand and in some cases eventually cause the businesses to fall apart. The warning signs came years prior, as soon as they began borrowing above their capacity to repay.

Debt is not a bad thing. Indeed, if you can borrow at 5% and use it to make 11%, it's good debt. It's a vehicle for making more profit. So I do not frown upon any companies using debt. However, if their interest on debt begins to exceed their capacity to repay that debt, then I will not touch them.

NET EARNINGS

After all the deductions from the revenue, how much is left for the board to reinvest or use for dividends? That's what net earnings are.

I'm pretty darn ruthless when it comes to net earnings. I want all my watchlist stocks to be making big profits relative to their size. That's why I focus on %. Again, you can look at the +£4 billion earnings BP made in 2019 and think wow. But when you see it's all that's left from £260 billion revenue, you realise they're not as efficient as you think.

Now, remember, we aren't looking for companies with the most profit. We want companies with the best chance of share price growth. In my experience that comes in-part from a solid net earnings %. How much are you keeping after deductions?

Companies with a 1% net earnings are too paper-thin. All it would take is a slight jump in expenses, or depreciation or a small drop in revenue and the company are probably going to be recording a loss.

Let me make it clear here that losing years will cause share prices to plummet. The opposite of what we are looking for as an investor in stocks. As a result, any company close to the edge of that are immediately dismissed from the criteria. They fail instantly.

All my CLEAN watchlist companies have superb net earnings figures. So high that they can probably weather any storm and continue to make significant profits. I do not want any losing years in my portfolio of stocks. The greater the margin, the better here.

LIQUIDITY

What assets do the company have? Are these growing or reducing each year? If so, what's going up precisely? Is it the inventory? Cash? Or perhaps it's accounts receivables going up? (the amount of money invoiced out but still waiting to be paid). What % of assets are attributed to accounts receivables? Are the company relying too much on unpaid debts being paid to them? If so, that's a concern.

Does the company have any property, plant and equipment? Are they investing in this area? What about intangible assets like rights, patents and trademarks? Do they have any long term investments? Are they selling off any significant assets?

What liabilities do they carry? Do they owe too much outstanding tax? How much do they owe their suppliers compared against how much they are waiting for from their customers? Do they owe more than what's coming in?

Do they have any debts that are due to be paid within the next year? Are any debts due to be paid within the next five years? Is the debt at a level where the company can pay it off? If so, how long would it theoretically take to pay it off? Is that timeframe acceptable?

All of these questions must be investigated and answered before I will consider a company for the watchlist. Everything must be stable on all of these factors and considerations.

Perhaps you are starting to understand why so many companies fail the test.

Overall, I want to see that the company have more assets on their books than liabilities.

Remember, assets generate income. For businesses, these might be inventory, property, vehicles etc. All are contributing to the income of the company.

Liabilities take money out of your pocket. These are debts, tax bills etc.

If liabilities outweigh assets, we have a problem.

RESERVES

The companies I pick love to pump profits into their cash reserves. I made this part of my criteria because it shows intent from the board. An intention not to pump all the profits into dividends but instead to grow the business.

I want to see consistent year on year growth of this figure. I want to see the business pumping more and more money into their reserves.

When you have a company making £40 million a year profit, but you know they are sitting on an available cash reserve of £500 million, you know the opportunities for growth are right there. They are poised, ready to take action when the opportunity comes. This tells me a lot about how a business is being run. It can lead to the chance to acquire a competitor and take them out of the game, building a larger moat around the business.

If anything it's a buffer for any tough times ahead. To me, it's a combination of security and potential growth. The amount they sit on isn't quite as significant. What I value more than anything is the consistency of adding to it.

The legendary martial artist Bruce Lee was once famously reported as saying "I fear not the man who has practiced 10,000 kicks in one day, but I fear the man who has practiced one kick a day over 10,000 days". It is a lesson in the importance of consistency.

Any company regularly, year on year, pumping money into their cash reserves has developed this as a habit. I think it is a very healthy habit to get into, and it is something I always look towards in my analysis.

BUYING BACK SHARES

Many of the watchlist companies are buying back their shares year after year.

This plays a vital role in driving up the share price.

When a company buys back it's own shares via a share buy-back scheme; it reduces the number of shares outstanding in the market. This concentrates the number of available shares and raises the demand for them. When there is more demand for a stock, its value often rises.

The process of a company buying back its shares can single-handedly help push a share price higher. Something I am very keen to happen to my portfolio of stocks. As a result, any company doing this gets a massive tick in my analysis.

Unlike many other factors already covered; however, it is not a pre-requisite for qualification to the watchlist. There are some companies in the watchlist that have superb results elsewhere but have not yet begun to buy back their shares.

This may be because the business has an alternative plan for growth, or perhaps they wish to reach a larger size before taking a percentage of their profits out for this purpose.

RETURN ON SHAREHOLDER EQUITY

How much does the business make in profit, based on the assets it has?

Put differently, what are the assets bringing in? This is a reliable measure of how well the board are putting the profits made to use. A company with a poor return on shareholder equity are investing in assets that are not producing much impact on the company profits. On the flip side, a company with a high return on shareholder equity are doing a fantastic job of purchasing assets that are contributing massively to the income being achieved by the business. The more efficient the assets being purchased by the business, the higher the score.

Every company I select for my portfolio has a track record of solid return on equity scores. This is an essential rule of thumb for me.

CONSISTENCY

One year of exceptional performance across all of these factors (and others) is not enough. I want to see consistency. I want to see that this way of operating is their usual way to do business. I am not interested if it's just a flash in the pan. I'm not interested if it's just a lucky year. I want to see that this is a way of business for them and has been for years.

As a result, any company I invest my capital into has to be showing all of these great results and be doing so for several years consecutively.

One good year of ticking all the boxes is not enough.

This can sometimes result in me being a little late to the party, something that can irk many investors. However, I would argue that I'd rather be sure about a company I'm investing in first of all.

I'd then afterwards point them to the results page in this book, which I think speaks for itself, no matter how late we may or may not be.

FINANCIAL SUMMARIES AND WHY I DON'T USE THEM

Robert Kiyosaki, author of 'Rich Dad, Poor Dad' has often been quoted saying "the reason investors think trading in stocks is risky is because they are taking massive risks!".

By massive risks, he means, they don't know what they're doing.

When you buy stocks without knowing why or what you're doing, you deserve to lose your money. It shouldn't be that simple, and quite frankly, it isn't.

The legendary investor Warren Buffet once said on a TV interview I watched that he believed that probably over 95% of investors do not read a companies financial statement.

It's astonishing just how lazy investors can be, evidenced by the now colossal supply of financial summaries which you can find on quite probably hundreds of websites out there in the digital world.

Financial Summaries are summaries of the companies financials. You can find these on Yahoo Finance, Tradingview and Marketwatch to name just a few of the hundreds out there.

They all give the same information, but they are designed to provide investors with a brief snapshot of information around the companies financials.

These summaries can be broken down over 2-5 years usually, but often three years seems to be the standard. They

[STOB] Stobart Group plc

Like most other FTSE constituents, Stobart Group plc did not make the grade and were immediately dismissed as an investment opportunity.

Since 2008, the numbers have not been strong enough. Expenses have been far too high over the last 10 years and in more recent times the depreciation costs have begun to grow as well.

Losing profits in 2014, 2015, 2017, 2018 and 2019 meant that my followers and I have managed to stay well clear of the downfall of Stobart Group plc's share price which fell from £2.70 a share in August 2017 to just £1.00 a share in 2019.

When investors are jumping in on this little FTSE Small Cap company because their profits jumped from -£9 million loss in 2017 to a +£100 million profit in 2018, I'm staying well away as I know whats happening behind the scenes. The financial numbers tell you everything you need to know, providing you know where to look and how to read them.

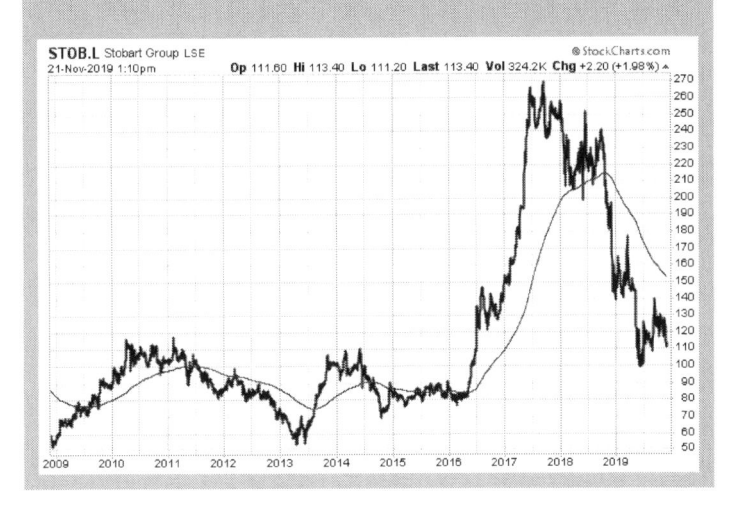

will show you the Revenue coming in over the last three years, the P/E ratios and several other one-off indicators that on their own tell us very little about what is going on.

Most investors use these summaries instead of putting in the hard work. They look at the companies EPS score (earnings per share), then look at the Revenue and maybe take a look at the P/E Ratio before making an investment decision.

No wonder people lose money and assume the markets are risky.

These financial summaries are of no use to me whatsoever. Why? Because they don't tell me anywhere near what I need to know to test a company against my criteria. Anyone using these summaries will miss vital information which can tell you what's truly going on at a company.

Allow me to provide an actual example here of the sort of information you miss using these sites.

Stobart Group plc are a FTSE Small Cap company with yearly Revenue of £146 million.

In 2018 they released their annual accounts and confirmed that they had made £100 million in net profit for the year.

This was no lie, and from a purely accounting perspective, the business did make that +£100 million profit.

However, as an intelligent investor, we must always look into what is going on behind the scenes. What is the source of income? Was it unexpected? Is it in line with the historical trend of previous years, or was it out of character for the business?

Regardless of these questions, I will always carry out a thorough analysis to uncover any underlying stories the numbers can tell me.

Stobart Group plc's numbers had a story to tell because that year (2018) the company had recorded a sale of assets to the tune of approximately £127 million.

The problem here is that despite it very much being income for the year from an accounting point of view, from an investment point of view it muddys the waters. You see, this £127 million income in 2018 from the sale of assets has nothing to do with the companies recurring business. To me, it is highly unlikely that Stobart Group plc will be able to sell off pieces of assets to that tune every year and maintain their £100m a year profit.

As an investor, I, therefore, want to omit this data. I have no choice to if I want to see the numbers for the underlying revenue of the business. I want to know what Stobart Group's everyday recurring revenue is. What's being generated by the everyday business they are running? Because this is what they'll be relying on in the future.

Yes, they technically made £100 million profit in 2018. But not from the everyday business.

When these extraneous income sources are removed from the results, it paints a very different picture. When investors are jumping in on this little FTSE Small Cap company because their profits jumped from -£9 million loss in 2017 to a +£100 million profit in 2018, I'm staying well away.

Because after removal of the assets they sold from their results it shows that Stobart Group plc made a -£28 million loss on the year from their everyday recurring business.

The story gets worse for them. As previous years also saw one-off assets being sold. In 2016 they sold £8.2m worth of assets. In 2017 they sold £6.8m worth of assets. All of this nothing to do with the underlying everyday business they operate.

So when you remove all of the extraneous income, this is what you are left with — the true picture of their performance.

YEAR	PROFIT
2012: £22m
2013: £0.7m
2014: -£11m
2015: -£10m
2016: £0.5m
2017: -£16m
2018: -£28m
2019: -£38m

Over these eight years, with all the years results combined, £96.7m was recorded as Stobart Group plc's accumulated profit.

However, with extraneous sales removed, the underlying recurring business actually achieved a total loss of -£81.4m over the same period.

Today news reports are being published that Stobart Group are in real trouble. Their share price has fallen from £3.00 a share in 2017, to £1.00 in late 2019. Banks are reportedly refusing to lend to the company any more. They see what might be coming here, I guess.

Emergency measures have reportedly been put in place at the company in a bid to save them, but most think it might be too late. Time will tell. However, I hope you can see just how easily investors can be misled by only reading

[COB] Cobham plc

This british aerospace & defence company from the FTSE 100 have had a rollercoaster of a ride in terms of their share price.

Between 2008 - 2014 things were going ok. They weren't qualifying for my portfolio, their results not being good enough to warrant inclusion. But they were a profitable business achieving around 8-9% net earnings a year.

I stayed away because quite frankly there were better companies to invest in at the time. These guys just didn't make the grade.

Then, in 2015 the company posted a losing year. A £37 million loss. The first major warning sign. This occurred despite a significant jump in incoming revenue that year. The cause however was a astronomical jump in expenses. From £504 million in 2014, to £651 million in 2015.

However, in 2016 it went from bad to worse as revenue fell, and expenses soared yet again. This time to the tune of £1.1 billion. This led to a final year -40.9% net loss. A staggering financial loss that year of £795 million.

It caused the share price to fall from £3.00 to £1.00 over the next three years.

summarised financial information.

The argument by most is *"well I don't have time to do all that number-crunching!"*.

Well, that's fine. But don't complain if you buy stocks in a company that on face value looked strong, but then just 2-3 years later have a share price at a 3rd of its level.

It's not the companies fault your being misled either. They are just doing what they are supposed to do by law. Financial reports are accounting documents. Every penny in and out must be accounted for. If they sell off a chunk of their business for £100 million, it 100% absolutely must be accounted for in the accounts.

It is up to the intelligent investor to use this information to disseminate the real facts from the data and work out what is going on. Otherwise, that investor will suffer some nasty surprises along the way and most likely be pumping his/her money into the wrong companies.

Cobham plc are a giant of the FTSE 100. One of the most popular stocks via my investment brokers website. A large percentage of their investor clients have positions held in Cobham plc.

Unfortunately, Cobham plc did not make the grade for my criteria. They were a long way away from ever making the grade.

In 2018 however, they reported their second year in a row of profits. 2017 saw an £84 million net profit. 2018 came in at £73 million. A little lower and a step in the wrong direction, but a profit nonetheless.

Of course, those figures are not enough for me. And indeed my 2-3 hours worth of analysis that I carried out highlighted

[SBRY] J Sainsbury plc

Operating in the highly competitive food retail industry J Sainsbury plc have spent the last 10 years scraping by. Like many of their close rivals such as Tesco and Morrisons, they take home a very thin slice of the pie each year.

At times resulting in net losses.

This is a business I would never invest in. It is too highly competitive, with very small margins and a terrible level of efficiency. In 2015 for example the business achieved a revenue of £23.7 billion. Impressive numbers for any business. Yet by the end of the year the company recorded a net financial loss of -£179 million.

It is this thin margin, coupled with a highly competitive industry that leads to such a volatile and inconsistent share price.

As can be seen from the chart below, Sainsbury's are trading at about the same level as they were 10 years ago.

Yes there have been ups, but these tremendous cliffs the price has repeatedly fallen off are largely attributed to the financials.

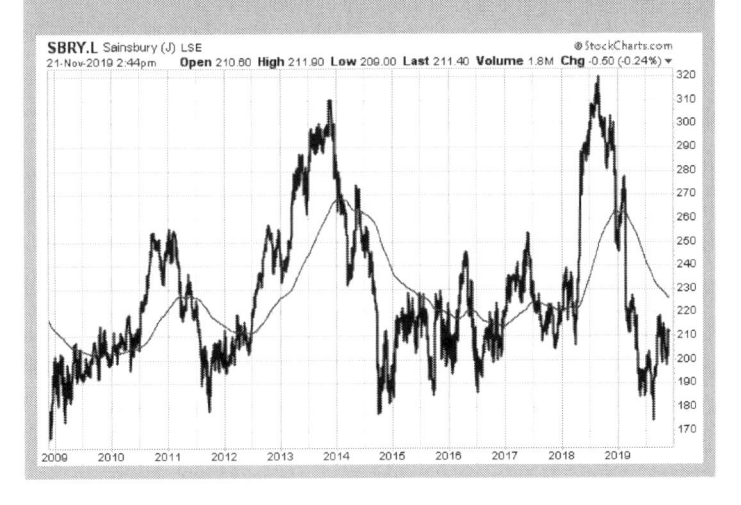

some serious issues. You see, that year Cobham plc received an income of £227 million. This was classed for accounting purposes as "profit on divestments".

Profit on Divestments means the profit made on sales of assets. Selling an asset might be the sale of rights, property, plant etc.

A quick look at the year before showed no income in this area. This was a one-off sale of assets that could not be counted upon year after year. It was nothing to do with the recurring revenue of the underlying day to day business.

After omitting this income from their financial results, a shrewd investor would find that Cobham plc actually would have suffered a -£153m loss that year. This would have been their 3rd losing year in the last four years.

A company I would not ever be investing in. Yet according to my broker, Cobham plc are one of the most popular stocks held by their clients.

Finally, my last example of the perils of skimming the financial data leads us to J Sainsbury plc.

The UK supermarket chain is a much-loved store and brand across the nation. However, struggling to compete in a highly competitive supermarket chain industry against rivals Tesco, Morrisons, Aldi, Lidl, Waitrose and US Walmart owned ASDA their numbers had been struggling for several years.

So, in 2016, they made the bold move to acquire the catalogue retail store Argos and promptly proceeded to install Argos collection points across their supermarket branches.

Having run my updated analysis on this business later on in

early 2019, I heeded a word of warning to my followers via my social media outlets. Sharing the critical financial data, I made it clear that not only did they still not qualify for my watchlist but that the numbers did not look pretty at all. 1500+ either read it and took it on board or thanked me for my insight.

However, one user quit my group in disgust and promptly made a song and dance about doing so. Clearly, some of us have a stronger passion for our supermarkets than I thought. It was a reaction more akin to what I'd expect had I punched his elderly mother in the face. Twice.

Two or three in the group pointed at me, effectively called me a blasphemer and told me to "stay out of it and stick to what you know". Whatever that meant. I thought it was clear that my trading and investing discussion group would involve some degree of discussion on ….well…..trading and investing. But ultimately they made it quite clear that they didn't care for what I was writing about their beloved Sainsburys.

Only one of the four complainants used any figures to question my analysis. Pointing to the revenue figures on a financial summary he had just found online he wrote "bullshit, Revenue going up year after year since the Argos acquisition! What rubbish Chris!".

This is a prime example of how skim-reading data will mislead investors into making poor investment decisions. He was right about the Revenue at least. It had been rising, year after year since the Argos acquisition in 2016.

2016: £23 billion
2017: £26 billion
2018: £28 billion

2019: £29 billion

But as explained earlier in this book, the Revenue does not give you much information about a business and how it is performing. If anything, the Revenue tells you that there is a growing market for what they sell and that people are going to them to buy it. It's the measure of how much money is coming in.

What revenue doesn't tell you is, how much the company keeps. And in this question lay the problem for J Sainsbury plc. Specifically, the company expenses.

Since the Argos acquisition in 2016, company expenses had risen to almost crazy levels.

2016: £850m
2017: £1.2 billion
2018: £1.4 billion
2019: £1.73 billion

The costs of running the business were accelerating faster than the growth in Revenue our friend was raving about, rendering that growth he was so excited about as worthless and adding no value. If anything, the rise in Revenue cost the business more profit as expenses rose with it.

This was more evident from the % of expenses growth relative to the gross profit being made.

2016: 58.4%
2017: 73.9%
2018: 75.2%
2019: 86.3%

In 2016 the cost of the expenses of the business took away 58.4% of the gross profit before taxes and other deductions. By 2019, just three years later, that figure had risen to 86.3% of the gross profit.

This ultimately resulted in declining profits for the business. Achieving £381 million profit in 2016, and in 2019 only making a £177 million profit.

Again in % terms relative to the revenue coming in, 2016 saw 1.6% of the incoming revenue kept as net profit. By 2019 this fell to just 0.6%.

Of all that £29 billion that came into the business, they only kept 0.6% of it as profit. That's one tight margin right there. A small jump in expenses or interest on debt could see them posting losing years. A slight increase in food costs? Or a small shift in customers moving away from Sainsbury to one of many different competitors could cripple them.

Indeed the share price also shares the same sentiment, as shrewd investors are staying away from this stock. Once high at £6.00, shares in J Sainsbury at the time of writing are down to £2.00 a share.

To wrap this chapter up, I want to make it clear that using financial summaries is not a wise move. Finding the right stocks to invest in takes work. It takes learning and understanding the nuances of the financials going on.

It takes a passion for knowing the truth and a keen eye for patterns and trends in the numbers. It takes a full understanding of what the numbers mean. Something I have gone some way to hopefully addressing a little in this book already.

However, I know that the reason many investors use these financial summaries is because they simply do not have the time or desire like I do to spend 2-3 hours on a company dissecting the data and identifying whether they should be invested in, put to one side to check again next year or kept well away from.

Many investors have lives to lead. They want a healthy return on their investment and are not willing to dedicate the time to all this.

I get it even though I cannot relate to it. I am an odd sort, you see.

I love sifting through these financial statements. Ask my partner, who will testify in any court that my obsession for company analysis often exasperates her. She has been known to wake up at 2 am to find me quietly punching numbers into a spreadsheet and working out the 2013 results for some FTSE Fledgling company no-one has ever heard of.

I get a genuine buzz from finding a small unknown company in the FTSE Fledgling index that meet the criteria or perhaps are so close that they'll qualify next year providing they improve ever so slightly. I get a real buzz from that.

I also get a similar buzz from crunching the numbers of the big corporate FTSE 100 giants and seeing just how bad things are behind the scenes. Stocks that many of my followers might have positions in because they trust the brand or only recognise the name. I love being able to share that data with them and give them a heads up that they may do better cutting their losses so far and putting that money elsewhere into far better stocks that I have found.

CHAPTER 7
THE WATCHLIST

THE**CLEAN**TRADER
STOCKPICKER REPORT

OCT 2019
Your exclusive fortnightly report providing you with the most exciting and promising stocks of 2019.

This week we take a look at a fantastic FTSE 250 company within the Industrial Support Services sector

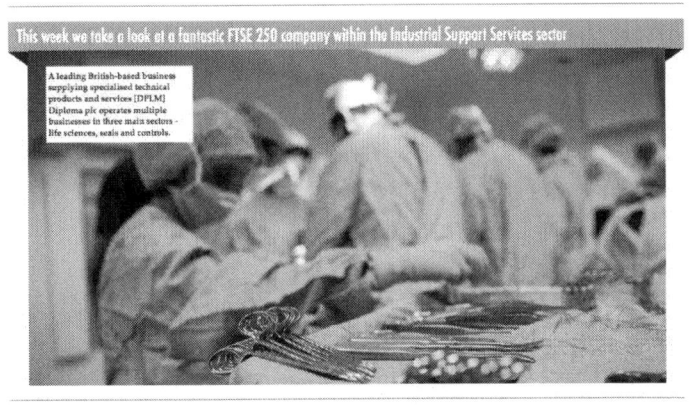

A leading British-based business supplying specialised technical products and services [DPLM] Diploma plc operates multiple businesses in three main sectors - life sciences, seals and controls.

Diploma plc [DPLM] Analysis Report

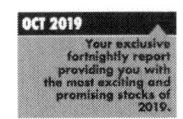

Expanding growth through acquisitions

Diploma plc [DPLM] supplies hydraulic cylinder seals and repair kits for excavator hydraulics as well as custom moulded machined seals, gaskets and filters. In addition to the seal industry DPLM also provide instruments for clinical diagnosis, products and services for blood, tissue and other sampling, medical equipment, products and services for hospitals and GI/Endoscopy units and clinics. 15% of revenue is also made up from providing analysing equipment, containment enclosures and emissions monitoring devices.

Diploma plc also has a Controls division responsible for 29% share of its yearly revenue. They specialise in wiring and cable components, fasteners, bearings, bolts, clamps and rivets to the aircraft, motorsport and aerospace markets.

The companies entry into these sectors was mainly achieved through acquisitions, starting in the UK and increasing their reach into other markets over time.

43% of DPLM's revenue comes from their Seals division

2018 in numbers

£54m
net earnings

£255m
held reserves

18.5%
return on shareholder equity

The CLEAN Stockpicker Report goes out to exclusive members twice a month, each issue highlighting one of the few rare companies that passed the CLEAN Watchlist criteria. Including financial breakdowns, dividend information and supporting information to explain why and how they successfully passed the grade.

THE CLEAN WATCHLIST

After developing my criteria and experiencing the results first hand, those close to me began asking me for tips and picks.

Historically this is something I'd never been keen to provide as I felt like a fraud. I genuinely believed that I didn't know any better than anyone else which stocks were going to do well. So who was I to be giving out picks? They were worthless in my eyes, much like many of the services out there today recommending companies as weak as QUIZ plc to their 100,000 followers.

If we are talking about which stocks will do well over the next day, week or even month then I STILL don't have this ability. I cannot make such predictions with any higher degree of accuracy than you could.

However, ask me which companies I think have the best odds of doing very well over the next 1-5 years+ and I'd say "yes!". Today I can stand up tall, hand on my heart and tell you with confidence exactly which companies are best geared to achieve an increased share price over that period, and what's more, I can provide factual evidence to back it up. No opinions here.

And so I started to help out my investor friends. Not only did I begin telling them the stocks I was buying, but I was telling them why. What was it about that company that was so good? Why did they beat the others on offer? What was it about their numbers that looked so strong?

Initially, these picks were word of mouth, or via What's App/Messenger, only I struggled to convey the accompanying information across with it.

I later began sending these out as very basic looking emails. No frills. Just the key information they needed.

In more recent times this has developed into a twice a month colour pdf magazine report, each issue covering another company from the watchlist. It contains all the critical financial information along with full write-ups from me on why I'm recommending them.

As soon as this began to get serious, and hundreds of people started asking to be involved, I began to charge £20 a month for these reports.

A meagre amount, but I wanted something in exchange for sharing the years I had pumped into learning what I knew. Couple that with the time it was taking to create this .pdf colour magazine twice a month. I also wanted to make sure subscribers felt like they were getting a huge no brainer return on investment from it.

At £20 a month, the access pays for itself. If you follow these companies and take action, you'll make the cost of the service back easy plus profit. Of that, I have no doubt. I can stand there with pride and say that. I know it to be true.

And so the CLEAN Stock Picker was born. A twice a month report straight into subscribers inboxes, for just £20 a month. Each issue covering a new company from my portfolio.

It was one of those win/win arrangements.

Investors want the returns but don't want to have to put in the work I put in. They don't want to have to learn how to read these financial statements and spend hours pouring over the data to interpret what it all means.

So let me do it for you? I'm already doing it for myself anyway.

Anyone today can get themselves access to this information, for less than half of the monthly cost of their morning coffees, and use that information to cover the cost and make significant returns on their invested capital.

I get paid something for my efforts. You get a massive return on your small investment.

A win/win deal as I call it. I love them.

If you are interested in learning more about subscribing to the CLEAN StockPicker service, you can do so by heading over to

https://thecleantrader.com/stockpicker

or email Chris for a chat at

chris@thecleantrader.com

CHAPTER 8
THE STRATEGY

MY STRATEGY

So by now, we should have a pretty good idea of how we pick out the best stocks available. This, of course, can work in any country. At the time of publishing, I'm about to start working on US and Australian stocks. I'm also considering exploring European stocks like the French and Belgian indices.

But how do we decide when to get into these stocks and when to get out? What system can a beginner adopt in order to make sure they get off on the right foot?

In this section, I will attempt to explain the approach and strategy that I use for my own long term investing.

BUY AND HOLD

This is the primary strategy I run, and it is the easiest and most straightforward of all the approaches. It works as it sounds. You buy the stock, and then you hold it. Anyone can do it.

This is far from a get rich quick scheme, however. In the last five years, this approach, combined with my stock picks, has achieved a growth of +163%. That equates to around 32.6% a year on average.

A £10,000 investment five years ago would today be worth £28,000 using this simple approach.

A £50,000 investment five years ago would be worth £140,000 today. If we happened to see another five more years of similar results, that amount would be worth £392,000.

The more you have in there, the faster it grows.

The aim here, however, is to accumulate income-producing assets. These assets (the stocks I own) produce income via dividends, but also through capital gains in terms of share price growth. I have no plans to sell these unless I wanted to or needed to. I allow them to grow in the background, raising my wealth and net worth over the years. I am also re-investing the dividends I am receiving into buying more shares in a bid to accelerate the growth.

As shown earlier in this book in the section COMPOUNDED INTEREST with regular additional monthly deposits this account can grow very well in 5-10 years.

> **ENTRY RULES**
> As soon as a company qualifies for the watchlist, I am free to buy shares in it.
>
> **EXIT RULES**
> If a companies financial performance falls out of the CLEAN watchlist criteria, i.e. it's latest report fails the test, then I am free to sell out my position in this stock and re-invest the capital into another more favourable opportunity.

I plan never to spend the money.

In 20 years, with £2500 a year additional investment (£200 a month for the next 20 years) I could be sitting on around £1.8m with yearly dividend income of £45000 aged 57. I may have more if the average dividend yield by then is higher than 2.5%.

However, more importantly, for me, I wish to pass this down to my children to manage. By which time they'll be around 25 years old.

By the time they're 30 they'll have a capital fund of £3.2 million. By 35 this will be £5.7m. By their 40's, once I'm around 75, this will be up to £10.3 million.

The yearly dividends at this point will be £207,000. That's a pretty solid retirement without even needing to touch the capital.

It would set my kids up for life, and their kids will probably be some of the wealthiest kids around.

All started by one man. Me.

No worrying about what price we get in at. We're buying more all the time. Some months you'll buy at expensive prices, others at low prices. Benjamin Graham called this approach "Dollar Cost Averaging".

The idea here is that instead of sitting on cash and waiting for the perfect moment to strike (that being when the price has fallen considerably, and shares are cheap) we buy our stocks like we buy our groceries — every month buying more and more.

Some months the prices are high. Other months they are low. Overall, you get the average cost which balances out. The main aim is to own the shares, regardless of the ever-fluctuating cost.

This particular strategy takes up almost no time if you subscribe to the watchlist and know the right stocks.

You read the reports, buy the stocks each month, and that's it. If you get paid a dividend one month, you use that money to buy more shares on top of your usual monthly purchase.

If you receive a heads up from me to say a company has fallen out of the watchlist, you sell and re-invest the returns elsewhere.

It's so simple, and you only need a laptop, broadband, a broker account, a monthly subscription to my picking service and about 15 minutes or so every two weeks.

No maintenance. No logging in every day to manage your stocks. It just does it's thing in the background. Each time you log in to buy more shares each month, you'll see it's performance.

GETTING IN AT THE RIGHT PRICE

Some investors want more precision when it comes to buying stocks in a company. They'll know the company they want to own shares in, but they only want to get in at the lowest possible price.

This can make you more profit if you manage to get it to work, but with that added benefit comes more work and more dedication as you will need to be checking the prices daily for any signs of opportunity.

Market crashes are a great time to buy more as it is much like going to the sales. All the prices are lower. However, to capitalise on this, you would need to store your cash and build it up without buying anything, waiting for that moment to come.

Otherwise, a market crash may appear, but you have already invested your money in other positions and don't have enough liquid funds to purchase all the stocks you want during the sale.

THE FEAR OF MARKET CRASHES

There's nothing that makes an investor's hair stand up on end than the consistent threat of an impending market crash.

Many people say we're due one. Others disagree. Some were saying this years ago.

When was the last crash we had? Well, it depends on what you call a crash.

In September 2000 the FTSE 100 fell 49% over 2.5 years, from 6798 to 3436. It then spent four more years heading back up before it reached 6798 again. A total of 6.5 years. It was called the 'dot com bubble'.

In September 2007 the FTSE fell 48% over 1.5 years, from 6657 to 3460. It then spent four more years heading back up before it reached 6657 again. A total of 5.5 years. It was called the 'sub-prime mortgage crisis'.

These were our two most significant crashes of the last 30+ years.

One took 6.5 years to go back to 'normal'. The other 5.5 years.

If you were an investor who had watched his account plummet 49% in value, you would probably be a step closer to imaging why people had famously jumped to their deaths after the stock market crash of 1987.

Yet just 6.5 years later or less, these crashes had fully recovered their losses and were now making gains.

Had those investors not sold at the worst possible time, and instead bought while these great stocks were super cheap to buy, they would have come out far more prosperous by the time the markets had recovered.

We have had crashes since though, albeit, far less intense.

In July 2011 the FTSE spent a month falling 21% in value from 6055 to 4791. It took another year and a half to recover.

In April 2015 the FTSE spent nine months falling 23%, from 7104 to 5499. It took ten months to recover.

These are relatively short recovery times. So even if you took no action over this period, after about 18 months, you'd be back up to where you were pre-crash.

However, these crashes are an opportunity for us — a chance to buy shares in fantastic stocks for a super low price. In fact, over a ten-month recovery period, you can buy more stocks once a month for ten months.

After the recovery is complete, not only are your original pre-crash stocks owned now back to their original value, but the extra stock you bought during the recovery are now flying and adding to your profits.

In other words, with the right mindset and attitude towards a crash, you can use them as an opportunity to grow your capital quicker than any other strategy.

They can be the best thing that ever happened to your portfolio.

Of course, if one particular company fails and goes to zero, you can lose your money. That's the frightening risk here.

However, the odds of that happening are significantly reduced when we are buying companies with substantial net profit margins and sitting on vast cash reserves.

There is a reason we are only buying shares in the best of the best. These companies will suffer the least during a crash, and they will recover the quickest on the way back up because they are doing everything right financially.

FACTORING IN COMISSION CHARGES

Commission is a significant consideration when starting with small capital. Accounts larger than £10,000 need not concern themselves too much with this, but sub £10,000 accounts will need to bear in mind the costs of buying stocks.

Many brokers charge a flat rate commission when you buy stock, and again when you sell a stock. This could be £5 to £10 per transaction.

This can play an essential factor if you have say £1000 to invest at the very beginning.

Assume we split the £1000 capital across ten different watchlist stocks, investing £100 in each stock. You would have to pay 10x commission charges to make those trades.

The beauty of a buy and hold strategy is you're not continually getting in and out of the markets. Therefore the transaction costs are vastly lower than that of spread betting or any shorter-term strategies.

You, therefore, would not pay another commission charge until you sold the positions.

However, different brokers have different rules and charges so you'd have to check with your broker of choice.

If after you opened your 10x positions you had another £1000 to invest a few months later, and you chose to split that across the same ten watchlist stocks, raising your position to £200 value on each company, you'd pay another

10x commissions. Depending on the cost this could create a £50-£100 fee. Bringing you down between -5 to -10% return already, just on commissions.

This is, therefore, a factor you must consider when purchasing your shares at the very beginning.

Also, note that some brokers charge an account fee of around £30 a quarter. Some have no charges at all, and others are more expensive. However, these companies also waive that charge if you have been active, buying three or more transactions in that quarter.

In essence, this means you're going to be charged for it anyway. So you may as well make three transactions a month, pay the commissions and get your account fee waived — a far better option than opening nothing and paying £30 for holding an account with nothing in it.

ASSET ALLOCATION

Many beginners I meet make the mistake of putting all their eggs in one tiny basket. They'll perhaps have say £6000 to invest and buy £3000 shares in Company A, and another £3000 in Company B.

The following month, after depositing their capital and putting it to work, they'll deposit another £250. They'll often then use that to buy £250 worth of shares in Company C.

Company A: £3000
Company B: £3000
Company C: £250

The problem here is that there is a bias. If Company C goes on to have a stellar year, but A & B have a non-growth year, then your account results will suffer.

As we are unable to predict which of the CLEAN Watchlist stocks are going to do the best between them, we need to come at this with a balanced risk approach.

Ideally, you want to own stock in all the watchlist companies in your portfolio, all with equal value invested.

A £14,000 account may have £500 each company split across the 28 constituents for example.

This means that you are putting equal weight on every stock. The right thing to do when you have no insight on which company is going to take off the most.

Of course, this is difficult to do when you're just getting

started. And so for those just starting, I say don't worry too much. However, once you have begun to establish your portfolio, keep an eye on your allocation.

Do you have more % of your capital tied up into one particular stock than another? If that stock happens to be the dud of the year, then you'll suffer for it.

Something I tend to do each year is take a look at this allocation of my assets and make maintenance adjustments. If one stock has too much value on it, I will consider selling some off, or bolstering those that are lower with next months deposit.

Again, depending on the size that you're playing at, you may well need to consider commission at this point.

Also, keep an eye on sector correlation. Often I will build my watchlist without too much (if any) correlation between stocks. Of course, they are all FTSE stocks (until we start work on the US and Australian list), so they are correlated in that way. However, I already try to avoid too many stocks from the same industry sector.

Too many media stocks, for example, may lead to issues for me if the media sector takes a hit one month. Instead of just taking the hit on one position, I'm taking it across three and ultimately costing myself more.

MY ASSET ALLOCATION RULE OF THUMB

Try to keep the amount you invest in each position consistent. Try to avoid putting too much emphasis on one position. Spread out the risk as best you can.

If you are starting small, say with £1000, consider picking just four stocks, splitting this up into four lumps of £250 per stock. Each time you have more to invest, try and stick to only £250 investment per stock. Once you have run out of new stocks to add, start raising your value on each one you hold. From £250 to £500, for example.

Yes, unbalanced asset allocation is inevitable when you get started. It gets easier once you are better established.

The best you can do is to remember not to put all your eggs in one stock and attempt to spread the risk as best you can while building your portfolio.

CHAPTER 9
THE SUCCESSES

THE SUCCESSES

I won't publish here all the stocks in the portfolio as it would devalue the subscription for the monthly reports I produce. It would be a bit of a kick in the teeth for my followers, and I'd be pretty miffed if someone did that whom I was following for picks.

Additionally, depending on when you read this, some of the stock picks you are about to read about may well have since come off the portfolio since going to press. They may no longer be one of the companies I own.

However, as incredible as it may seem, these examples provided are typical of the 27 stocks in my portfolio. You will notice a stark contrast in share price growth to companies like BP, Sainsbury's, Cobham and Stobart Group, for example.

By identifying the rare few stocks that meet my criteria, I have successfully achieved a 96% success rate in finding stocks whose share prices rise once they make the grade.

Only one stock [OTB] On The Beach plc has failed to rise in value since passing the criteria and being added to the portfolio.

They passed in October 2018 when their share price sat at £5.00 a share. Today this sits at £4.37. A drop of -12% over the last year. It is still early days for them, however, as I usually go in with a five-year outlook at least, unless the forthcoming financial reports suggest otherwise.

To the charts then......

[HLMA] Halma plc

Halma plc is a global group of life-saving technology companies that make products for the hazard detection and life protection industries. They registered as a public limited company in 1981.

Having analysed their accounts covering 2008-2019, I was sufficiently impressed. I rarely find a company that tick all the boxes of my criteria and these guys had been doing it successfully year on year since 2009.

Consistent revenue growth, well-controlled levels of debt, strong net earnings, assets growing faster than liabilities, cash reserves consistently growing from £156 million to £810 million and excellent stats comparatively beating most of the FTSE 100 constituents put these guys high up on my watchlist.

Halma plc officially qualified for the CLEAN Watchlist following the release of their March 2009 earnings. Back then, the price was £1.60 a share. Today that share price is £21.00. That's an 1170% growth. Over the last five years since I've been actively investing this strategy, we've seen a 245% growth on this stock.

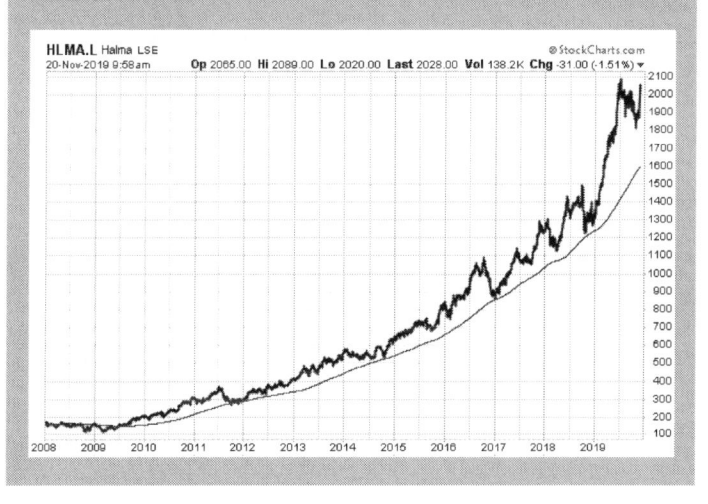

[SGE] Sage Group plc

Accounting software firm Sage Group plc was one of my earliest acquisitions.

Since 2007 this business has run to astonishing efficiency. A consistent yearly increase in revenue, high margins and acceptable levels of expenses mean this company are keeping a relatively large slice of the pie in comparison to other FTSE constituents.

A healthy asset investment plan and a focus on building cash reserves mean I've been a big fan of this £1.8 billion revenue business.

Qualifying for the watchlist on 3rd October 2011, Sage Group plc's share price back then sat at £2.52. Today this sits at £7.50 a share at the time of publishing.

Approximately +200% rise in share price growth over the last eight years.

The stock has seen a +24% increase in share price so far in 2019.

[DPLM] Diploma plc

A leading British-based business which operates multiple companies in three main sectors - life science, seal and controls. This constituent of the FTSE 250 qualified for my portfolio in October 2012.

A healthy gross margin and some of the lowest expenses relative to revenue that I've seen all help to achieve their excellent net earnings figures. The last ten years have also seen the company pay off almost all of its outstanding debt.

Consistency is the keyword here with Diploma plc. Revenues going up every year for the past ten years show the industry is strong. Net earnings rising every year show you can rely on this company for good results.

These guys are superb at investing in the right areas too. Assets outweigh liabilities by 2.0x and reserves are being pumped into every single year. The return on shareholder equity shows that the assets being bought are contributing well to the earnings, and the company are also buying back their shares.

Just look at that share price growth the past ten years too!

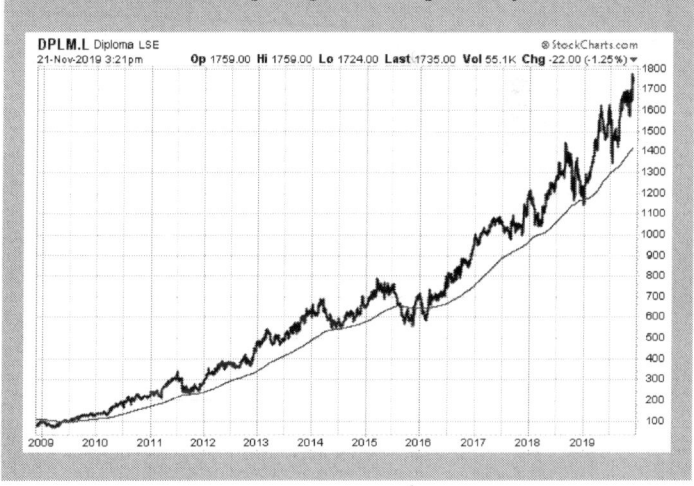

[GLE] MJ Gleeson plc

Homebuilder MJ Gleeson plc has only posted eight years of numbers since floating on the markets back in 2011. Yet their numbers have been impressive since 2012 onwards. It took them another year to qualify for the portfolio via my criteria.

Back then, their share price sat at £3.26. Today that figure sits at £8.16 just six years later — a growth of 150%.

This share price has risen +32% alone in 2019.

Again, this company had all the hallmarks you would come to expect of a company I'm investing in. Growing revenue, growing margin, reducing expenses. All of these trends appearing over eight years. Debts are non-existent, and the earnings are superb.

Assets also outweigh liabilities by 4.7x, which is huge, and this company are increasing reserves by +10% a year.

Another classic CLEAN Stockpicker company.

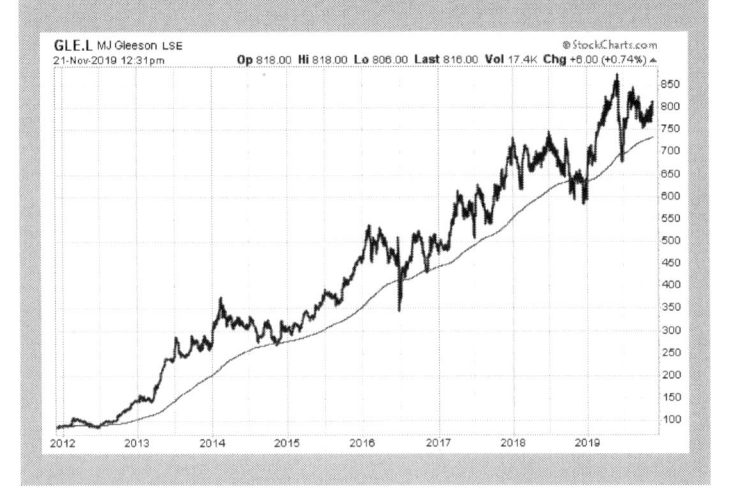

[ABDP] AB Dynamics plc

AB Dynamics is a small, relatively unknown UK supplier of integrated test systems for the global automotive industry. Their products are integral to the development and testing of tomorrow's motor vehicles — their equipment used by 25 of the worlds largest vehicle manufacturers.

I first learned of AB Dynamics from a tip-off from a subscriber Jaymie Duncan who asked me to take a look at the numbers against my criteria. Sure enough, the tip-off was great. ABDP smashed my criteria and passed the test. They were accepted into my portfolio from September 2014.

Back then, the share price sat at £1.64.

Since then, they have run with a superb margin, and the lowest expenses ratio I have seen yet. All achieved with no debt. They have some of the best earnings I've seen relative to revenue, and I'm incredibly impressed with the numbers. Remember, passing my criteria is very rare. These guys did it with ease.

The impact on the share price? Today it sits at about £27.30. That's a rise of 1565% in share price value over just five years.

CONTACT THE AUTHOR

Thank you, then for reading this book. I genuinely hope you have found it as it was intended. An eye-opening and insightful look into the simplicity of shrewd investing in stocks.

I built my criteria for stock selection purely selfishly, to aid my own investments and net worth. However, I have come to love sharing my work with others who appreciate it, hence why I decided to write this book to help others looking to embark on a similar journey.

If you wish to get involved in the CLEAN Stockpicker service I provide you can do so by heading to my website and signing up.

https://thecleantrader.com/stockpicker

If you would like to chat to me, either to say hi or ask any questions, I warmly welcome it and you'll find me open for business and open to discussion. You can get hold of me in a couple of ways...

EMAIL
chris@thecleantrader.com

WEBSITE
https://thecleantrader.com

FACEBOOK
https://facebook.com/chris.chillingworth

Trade safe,
Chris Chillingworth